So, You Think You're Alone

My dearest Father

Its done!

The future of this
work is in your hands
I love you
with all my heart
& soul.
Your
Annie

Lord
I put everything I
had I am in this work &
Done in my deepest Love

Thank-You for holding me
lovingly in Your hands
Thank You for having faith in
me
when I
don't have
faith in myself

I Am & will always Remain
Your child.

I now share Your work
through me, with the World

So, You Think You're Alone

Ann Marlatt

www.soyouthinkyourealone.com

Seraphina Press
212 3rd Avenue North, Suite 570
Minneapolis, MN 55401
612-455-2293
www.SeraphinaPress.com

ISBN - 0-9798246-0-5
ISBN - 978-0-9798246-0-9
LCCN - 2008928075

Book sales for North America and international:
Itasca Books, 3501 Highway 100 South, Suite220
Minneapolis, MN 55416
Phone: 952.345.4488 (toll free 1.800.901.3480)
Fax: 952.920.0541; email to orders@itascabooks.com

Cover Design by Pam Sepesi
Typeset by Peggy LeTrent

Printed in the United States of America

Dedication

To my husband John, who completed his part of our mission together, with loving success; and to my children and grandchildren who have been the inspiration for me to finish.

Contents

Author's Note

Many years ago during an extraordinary visit from the "other side" and following his earlier near death experience, my husband John was told that he and I had agreed to come to this earth to experience and complete a mission that would ultimately affect many lives. The experience left John with insightful mental abilities which he did not understand and really frightened him. Every logical sense in my body fought to believe that any of this could be true. The feeling that we had been "picked out" to complete some kind of spiritual responsibility was just too far reaching for my mind to believe and left me doubting that anything like that could happen. In strong denial after his death, I put aside the idea that I could have been a part of such a mission but the thought that I came here with a predetermined plan haunted me. Healing was painfully slow but the miracles in my life continued and, one day, inspired me to seek out the answers I needed to fulfill my life's work. My quest for the truth brought me to the realization that there was a much deeper meaning for life that existed beyond what I could see, feel or even imagine, and an infinite universe of unseen helpers have always been there waiting to assist and guide me. So, You Think You're Alone is a story of the unseen helpers in our lives. Collectively, the many short stories establish the existence of spiritual entities who walk with us each day, ready to help when we set our logical thoughts aside and reach out to what is unseen and very real. The spiritual interventions go beyond what our human senses can detect and reach to that part inside of us that is searching for truths that are beyond reason.

People are seeking reasons to believe in a loving, caring God during the darkest hours of their lives. We all look for inspirational examples of a spiritual existence especially in difficult times. This book deals with very real, human challenges with very real "Spirit" intervention. The stories do not demonstrate that things will always end the way we had hoped, but makes it clear that you will never be alone when you are dealing with things you don't understand.

Looking back I realize that my journey really began at a time even before my birth in the early 1940's. Spiritual interventions in the lives of my father and mother marked the beginning of events that would lead me towards a destiny that shaped my life into something much different than I had planned for myself. Initially my profession as a registered nurse happened in spite of me and not because of something I wanted to do, but it evolved into a very deep and rewarding part of my life. My career led me in many different directions in the field of nursing from caring for children in pediatrics to nursing supervision and more, but now I find myself called to work with the terminally ill and their families in hospice.

The biggest blessing in my life has always been my family. John and I were married for nearly 34 years before he died. We had four children and eleven grandchildren. As I watch the years unfold before me I realize that the spiritual thread that began with my parents and ran through my life has continued to wind through the lives of my children and grandchildren, touching and shaping things that will lead to the next generation and then the next. The completion of this book marks the end of the mission that began more than 60 years ago between John and me, and opens the door for my next journey to begin. I am an ordinary woman that was set on an extraordinary path in life.

Acknowledgements

My deepest appreciation and gratitude to Pam Sepesi, my friend and graphic designer, who put so much love and talent into helping me make this book a reality.

Frankie
Grandson

Robert
Grandson

Cristy
Granddaughter

Andrew
Grandson

Joshua
Grandson

Justin
Grandson

Joseph
Grandson

Zachary
Grandson

John
Grandson

Alexis
Granddaughter

Kayla
Granddaughter

John
Son

Cathy
Daughter

Sandra
Daughter

Frank
Son

John Marlatt
Husband

Ann Marlatt
Author

Joan
Sister

John Marlatt
Father

Thelma Marlatt
Mother

Marie Fielder
Mother

Frank Fielder
Father

Elsie Raye
Aunt

Dora Robinson
Grandmother

Frankie
Grandson /
Adopted

Robert
Grandson /
Son of Frank

Cristy
Granddaughter /
Daughter of Cathy

Andrew
Grandson /
Son of Sandra

Joshua
Grandson /
Son of John Jr.

Justin
Grandson /
Adopted

Joseph
Grandson /
Son of Sandra

Zachary
Grandson /
Son of Cathy

Little John
Grandson /
Son of Frank

Alexis
Granddaughter /
Daughter of Cathy

Kayla
Granddaughter /
Daughter of Sandra

John Jr.
Son of Ann and John

Cathy
Daughter of Ann
and John

Sandra
Daughter of Ann
and John

Frank
Son of Ann and John

John W. Marlatt Sr.
Husband of Ann

Doras "Ann"
Fiedler Marlatt
Author

Joan
Sister of Ann
(Frank III & Grover R.
brothers not pictured)

John E. Marlatt
Father of John W.

Thelma Marlatt
Mother of John W.

Marie Fielder
Mother of Ann

Frank Fielder Jr.
Father of Ann

Elsie Fielder Raye
Aunt of Ann

Dora Robinson
Maternal Grandmother
of Ann

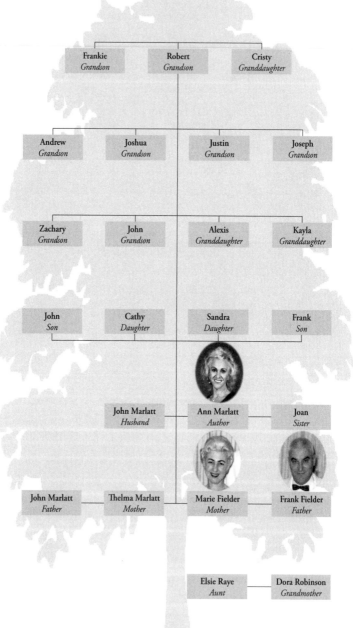

| Frankie | Robert | Cristy |
| *Grandson* | *Grandson* | *Granddaughter* |

| Andrew | Joshua | Justin | Joseph |
| *Grandson* | *Grandson* | *Grandson* | *Grandson* |

| Zachary | John | Alexis | Kayla |
| *Grandson* | *Grandson* | *Granddaughter* | *Granddaughter* |

| John | Cathy | Sandra | Frank |
| *Son* | *Daughter* | *Daughter* | *Son* |

| John Marlatt | Ann Marlatt | Joan |
| *Husband* | *Author* | *Sister* |

| John Marlatt | Thelma Marlatt | Marie Fielder | Frank Fielder |
| *Father* | *Mother* | *Mother* | *Father* |

| Elsie Raye | Dora Robinson |
| *Aunt* | *Grandmother* |

Story One

It was a time of war, World War II. Frank had been drafted then transferred into the Navy because of his knowledge and skills in electronics. He spent some time at Notre Dame for officer's training, went to Harvard and M.I.T. for training in the field of radar, and became one of only a hand-full of men who would hold a special radar officer classification. As the time neared for his graduation and the holidays approached, Frank and Marie shared a dream to be together for Christmas but it seemed out of the realm of possibility.

I wanted so much to be with him, Marie said. I couldn't even imagine how we would get the funds together. I worked for Wells Aircraft; it was what a great many of us were doing to help the war effort. Grandma and Grandpa tended the two boys at home. Frank III was the youngest and Frank had yet to see him since his birth months before. One evening at break time my co-workers gave me a sandwich filled with the kind of lettuce that made my dreams come true- cash! It wasn't long after that I found myself on a train headed for Boston. The train was filled with soldiers and sailors. I thought about how the war had changed so many lives. An old pot bellied stove sat in the middle of the car to warm us on a very cold and snowy mid-December journey. "There he is," I beamed excitedly, as the train pulled into the Boston station. Just holding him seemed like heaven to me. I realized even more how much my heart ached for him over the past few months.

We were soon on our way to his rooming house. The landlady was a very kind woman who rented many rooms in her home to servicemen. After reaching the house, he had to go back to school, leaving me with the afternoon free to wander about on my own. I jumped on the bed and thought how great it felt to be there. My thoughts wandered to the situation in the world. I dismissed the thought that this might be the last Christmas we would share; I didn't want those thoughts to ruin our time together. I got up and asked the landlady for directions into town. I wanted to surprise Frank with a Christmas tree all set up and decorated when he arrived home that evening. It was freezing out there as I picked up the tree and headed back to the room. I got hopelessly lost for a time but finally found my way back. I decorated the little tree and then put a present or two under it. Totally exhausted now from the journey and all the excitement, I fell into bed in a sleep that would last for two days.

Christmas came and went and we found ourselves in early January. It would soon be time to part. His graduation brought with it new orders. He was to go to Texas for still more training and I would be going back to our family in California. The train we boarded would allow us to travel together until he reached his destination in Texas.

The time on the train was filled with laughter and shared memories of times gone by. As the train moved through Indiana, I thought of my aunt who lived in Lafayette, which brought back other memories in my life. I suddenly got homesick to see her. We had some time left before Frank needed to report in Texas so I asked him if we could get off the train and take a bus to visit with my aunt when it pulled into the next station.

It sounded like a great idea to me, said Frank, that is until we got off that train. Snowdrifts were piled up three feet high and more along the sides of the road. I wondered at this point what possessed us to make this little side trip. It was just so cold. We found our way to the bus headed for Lafayette, climbed on board, and sat close to each other to keep warm. As we headed down the road a strange sense came over me. Maybe something just didn't sound or feel right, but I was sure that we would never make it to Lafayette on this bus. Before long, my fears were realized when the bus just stopped dead. Without so much as a word the driver opened the door, got off the bus and walked away leaving a bus full of bewildered passengers wondering if he was ever going to come back. "Well, guess we just have to wait," I chuckled, but we were both just happy that we were together no matter where we were.

We noticed the nun behind us on the bus when we boarded. She got up from her seat now and walked to where we were sitting to speak to me.

"Excuse me, sir, do you have the time?" Anxious and unsettled that we were stranded there, she thanked me and returned to her seat. A few moments later, becoming more and more disturbed that no help had arrived, she asked for the time again. Her level of anxiety seemed to be growing by the moment so when she walked to us for the third time, I asked her if I could help.

"Yes," she said. "If you could, please go and find a phone and call a priest I know in the next town. I know he will come pick me up if you could only get in touch with him."

How could I ignore her plea? I really didn't want to go for a walk with that thick blanket of snow on the ground. I was wearing only my summer khakis and I didn't look especially forward to freezing my behind off. Still, I really wanted to help her, so out I went to find a phone. "Wow, it's really cold out here," I thought as I walked away from the bus.

I nearly missed the little old gas station about a half mile or so up the road, it was so buried by the snow. Inside there was a hand full of old boys chewing the fat and minding the store. "Mind if I use your phone?" I asked.

"Sure! You go right head," one of them hollered out.

I picked up the receiver and cranked that old phone till the laughter in the place stopped me cold. "I can't seem to get this thing to work," I yelled out. By this time those old boys were just knee-slapping happy over my dilemma.

"Hey young feller," one of them shouted, "hang it up and then crank it!" I heard someone say something about them "city boys" but already red-faced I choose to just get this over with. A man answered when I called the number and told me that he would be right there. I hiked my way back to the bus, happy to be able to tell the nun that her ride was on the way. To my astonishment by the time I returned that priest was already pulling up in a brand new Nash.

He came on to the bus and helped the sister to the car. They started to drive away and then suddenly stopped and backed up. "The sister sends her apologies and wants to know if we can drop you off somewhere," said the priest. We were happy to find a way out of this dilemma and gladly accepted the offer. As we piled into the back seat the priest proudly stated, "It's brand new, just took delivery of this baby today."

That little car and that priest gave us the ride of our lives. He had one speed -fast. We skidded across bridges and slid down roads. Finally the priest pulled into the parking lot of St. Elizabeth Hospital and skidded to a halt. The small talk stopped and suddenly the mood in the car changed to a more serious nature. The nun reached into the cloth bag that she had been carrying and brought out a quarter-sized cloth medallion. She turned to me and looked straight into my eyes. She spoke softly and slowly, "My son, I just came from Rome where the pope himself blessed this little medallion. I want you to have it. Keep it with you always, for it will protect you. You and your family will always be blessed." We were very puzzled, but very grateful. It was just something in her eyes. The nun exited the car and bid us goodbye. The priest said that there was no time to spare for her, but now he could drop us off at our destination.

He later explained that she was a surgical nun flown in from Europe to assist in the operating room. They would be doing surgery on a catholic dignitary at 6:00 p.m. and they would not wait another moment for her to arrive. It seems he now drove at a more normal pace, and before long was bidding us goodbye and well wishes. We thanked him for the ride and waved as he drove out of sight. We stood in silence for a time then turned toward each other and began to laugh. Yes, it seems to have been a very unusual day indeed.

Our time together seemed to pass so quickly, said Marie, and soon it was time for another sad goodbye. We parted in Texas and I came home to be with our children in California. The months passed and eventually the news came. Frank was being sent to San Diego, California. This would be the last stop for him before going out to war. He would join a squadron on an unknown ship with a charted course into destiny. We met in San Diego for the last time before his departure. There was to be a party, a farewell dinner aboard the ship, and all the wives of the men from the squadron had been invited. Frank explained to me that they were given permission for the wives to come onboard as long as we didn't learn the name of the ship. Great care was taken to ensure that none of us found out. Every trace of the ship's name was covered or removed in some way to prevent us from finding out, but they forgot to cover the Commission Plaque that was in front of our faces when we walked aboard the vessel. It was the USS Bismarck Sea, a small aircraft carrier. It would be going out to sea as part of the Pacific fleet. I remember feeling the fear that thousands of us felt in those days -would I ever see him again? I cried as our last night together came to an end. We reminisced about the precious times we shared when we could be together in the past few months. We spoke about that day that we decided to step off the train and take that side trip to my aunt's. What in the world ever possessed us to do that? We laughed. "Do you have the gift that she gave you?" I inquired. Frank pulled out his wallet and showed me the medallion given to him by that nun, tucked in between the pictures of our children. How I prayed that God would return him safely to us. Our final farewell left me with another surprise - a child would be born into this world in a few months.

The carrier sailed off into the Pacific towards Hawaii, Frank said. You lose track of time when you are on board; one day is the same as the next. I don't even recall the first battle that we encountered, but our first casualty was a flight pilot who crashed coming in for a landing. The pilot always had a fear of flying, and now fate took him as the first casualty of our vessel. Times fluctuated between boring and tense. The sight of the first bomber swooping down on us was something I will never forget. It was a nerve-racking time for me because I really had no battle station. When the fighting started, I was usually up out of the way. My work was mostly done at night. I flew occasionally but mostly on reconnaissance missions. We dropped a bomb or two but that was the extent of it. It was my responsibility, and that of my crew, to keep the planes' radar and electrical systems functioning. When the planes landed, we began our work. We had to have all aircraft flight-ready by 4:00 a.m. each day. We were deeper and deeper into this war. I remember the sight of the first kamikazes we encountered. How vulnerable I suddenly felt as the ship next to ours sunk after being attacked by these suicide bombers off the coast of the Philippines.

The days turned into weeks, the weeks into lonely months and before long it was Christmas Eve. In my sadness and longing I wrote home:

My Dearest Darling Wife,

Darling, last night I intended to write you another letter. I couldn't write, dear, for my mind was thinking and thinking of how I need you and I was so very, very blue. At 7:30 p.m. we had a party aboard ship. I didn't want to go but it was more or less an order that we attend. I am now not sorry I went, for it turned out to be far different than I expected. The Chaplain organized the party and the word "party" turned out to be very misleading. It was a service. The Chaplain took charge and he knew what was in the heart of every man aboard the ship. He started by recalling the first Christmas from his Bible. It really touched the hearts of the men. He then led us in prayer and prayed for an early return to the states. A few presents were then passed out after which, to me, came the most beautiful part of the evening. The Chaplain gave a prayer for all our loved ones back home. Darling, I could never describe that moment. At the completion of his prayer, not a sound was heard for what seemed like an eternity. From off in the distance a bell could be heard ringing. How I wish I could describe those few moments. If I could put my heart in writing, I would describe it. Marie, the Chaplin we have aboard is a great man. He knows what we aboard think of and want most. After the services were over the Captain of the ship got up and claimed our Chaplain to be one of the greatest men he had ever known. I was sitting near the front and I am sure I could see tears in the captain's eyes. Truly dear, it was the most beautiful service I have ever seen. Darling, I shall never know Christmas again till we are once again together. I hope and pray for each day to fly by till I can be home with you. I hope our children had a lovely Christmas. I hope they knew the joys that Christmas should bring to them. But tell them that their daddy was sorry he couldn't be there with them. I have to close for now. I prayed for you and our family and I shall pray for you tonight. God bless you and remember I love you dearly.

With all my love, Frank.

The date was February 21, 1945. We were off the coast of Iwo Jima. The battles had been raging for two days. The Saratoga took a beating under attack. The enemy wanted the big ships. The Saratoga was a big carrier and they really went after her. Some of her planes landed on our little carrier, not able to get back to her deck. Together with other destroyers, cruisers, battleships and carriers, it was the USS Bismarck Seas' role to cover the invasion of the island. The Navy planned to continuously bombard the island. We hoped to soften it up and make the landing of the Marines a lot easier. Our planes' job was to take off from the carriers, fire on the island, and return for more fuel and ammunition. It was getting dark and the last planes were in from the day's job. The pilots reported that they had not seen any enemy planes while they were out, but we were later to learn that 60 or more aircraft had been in the area. A handful of us was given permission to go to the galley and grab something to eat. Many of us hadn't eaten all day. The Captain warned, "If you hear anything - anything at all-get out of there quickly. Every door between compartments will be locked down at the first signs of trouble; you will be trapped in there."

Tired and worn from the day's fighting we slipped down to the galley. It was strangely silent as we set to getting something to eat. Suddenly there was a flicker in the lights. Maybe it was nothing, but without conversation, or hesitation, we ran to the hatch above the kitchen. A suicide plane swooping low over the water hit a section of the fan tail beam and started a fire. The crew raced to put out the flames but the water supply was part of the damage that the bomber created. Another problem ensued- the ammunition was firing. The fire crew was dodging the fire from the exploding ammo, yet they continued to try to extinguish the flames. The fire attracted another suicide bomber. The glow of the fire reflected from the elevator shaft and gave him the advantage he needed to dive directly into the open elevator-well, killing and injuring all of the fire-fighting party and wiping out a repair party. Men were yelling, "Get to the hanger deck!"

Fear and yet order prevailed among the men. We got to the hanger deck just before the second plane hit. Afterwards the whole deck exploded. The fire and explosions had created an inferno that began to ignite the bombs and fuel in the planes that were close by. Ammunition exploded all around us. Men fought their way to get to the flight deck. We were shoulder to shoulder on the ladders to the deck. The air was filled with the terror of men struggling to survive. The explosion was deafening. The growl and the violent shaking that occurred as the next explosion hit was beyond description. I blinked, it seemed only for a split second, but when I opened my eyes, I was alone. We were like sardines struggling to get to the flight deck, and now I was totally alone. "Oh God," I cried out. "So many gone, they're all gone." I had no time to think, I just kept going. Suddenly, even in the struggle for my life, a sense of peace engulfed me. Where it came from, I cannot explain. Some how I knew I would be alive when this was over.

I reached the flight deck. The entire ship was burning; the heat was intense. There was fire everywhere. I took off running to my life station. Something caught my eye as I raced past. I paused only for the briefest moment as I recognized what remained of the ship's Chaplain. I later learn that he had offered one last battle prayer that the ship's company would have the skill to save our ship, our planes and ourselves from the hands of evil. I was in charge of getting that life-raft into the water. When I got to my life station, a group of men were there waiting for me to launch the raft. "There, it's loose," one of them said. "God, now it's hung up on something."

I slid down the rope and struggled to get it into the water. The intense heat of the fire took its toll on the mortally injured, battered and beaten body of that carrier. I could never even come close to describing the noise as, at that moment, she blew apart in one giant horrendous explosion. A moment before there was a flight deck and now it was nowhere to be seen. I looked up only to see that all the men waiting for me to launch the raft were gone. I am not sure of their fate; they were just gone. I fought to get that raft into the water. I was alone again, hanging onto the rope on the side of the ship, still trying desperately to free it up. Something came crashing down on top of me and it knocked me into the water. The hope of getting the raft into the water was gone.

My life vest was on backwards. I tried over and over again to inflate the other side, not realizing I was blowing into the side that was already inflated. The sea was cold, rough, and unyielding. Waves battered us and crashed ten feet, twenty feet and more over the top of us. Men screamed in fear to be rescued. Many were lost, fighting the waves that were relentless that night. How thankful I was to have spent many days of my youth body surfing in the ocean. I knew fighting the waves was useless. I let the water crash over me and then floated up to the surface. Still it was exhausting. Fear continued to overtake so many. There were rafts in the water and some men were able to climb aboard them. The sea appeared to be covered with the twinkling of fireflies as the small flashlights that were carried by the survivors signaled their locations. The enemy planes were still in the area; we were still targets. They began strafing us relentlessly. Many men were lost as the low-flying planes unloaded their deadly rounds of gunfire onto the survivors who were fighting for life in the water. The life rafts became the best targets. Others were trying to swim to destroyers that were running searchlights for survivors. You could hear the panic, screaming and crying. You could hear machine guns. I tried to stay calm as the minutes turned into hours, each hour feeling like an eternity; and then watched in terror as I realized that the fleet began to move away.

The Destroyer Edmonds fell back from the fleet and continued the rescue efforts. We would learn later that her skipper, Captain Burroughs, was sent a message by the Admiral to rejoin the fleet that was now several miles away or face disciplinary action, up to and including court martial. "Send over a flare and get out of there," he was told. He said he turned and glanced over towards what was left of the little carrier. The fuel and oil from the ship was burning and the whole ocean was in flames. The fire from the burning ship was the biggest flare he had ever seen. He told his crew that he could not fathom leaving even one of the men stranded in the cold unyielding sea as they were crying out from a certain watery grave. He said that the explosion created by the destruction of the USS Bismarck Sea was so horrendous that his teeth were aching. "I'll not leave these men to die," was the message sent back to the admiral.

He looked into the sea and promised to pull every survivor out of those waters. The destroyer would push forward upwind of us, turn off her engines and drift back among the survivors. Cargo nets and ropes were thrown to the men. Most of the men were just too exhausted to climb up out of the water. Many were pulled up onboard out of the nets and some just couldn't hold on. They fell back into the sea. The waves were so high a vacuum was created as the ship rose and fell on the waves, and they were drawn beneath the vessel. The destroyer finally drifted into my location. I reached for the rope hanging off her side. I caught it. I wrapped it around my waist. I could feel them pulling me up out of the cold stormy sea finally to safety. I was alive. I was not even injured- not one drop of my blood was spilled. Crewmembers pulled me aboard and held me from each side. I asked where to go as the crewmembers tried to assist me. Too proud, I told them to let me go. "Sir, but sir," they pleaded once, twice, even four times.

Too stupid, this time I ordered them to let go of me. Like a water-soaked tree in the wind I went down face first to the deck. I was taken to a room with a cot to lie down. I was so cold and wet and now a bloody mess. The men brought me a pair of dry pants; it was the only clean clothing available on board. I remember feeling water-logged. I lay there contemplating the events of the day till I regained enough strength to get out of those wet bloody clothes. I reached for my pocket to remove my wallet but it was gone. I looked at my hand. My wedding ring was gone, but my watch was on my wrist. I looked at the time. It read 7:06 p.m. It must have stopped when I hit the water. I thought how that angry sea claimed some of my most treasured belongings, but thank God, I was safe.

Slipping out of my wet pants, my hand brushed across a small lump in the back pocket. "What in the world is this," I thought, as I searched through the pocket. I gasped in disbelief. I stared at it in total amazement. My thoughts went back to that moment in time when a little nun looked me straight in the eyes. I remember the strange feeling I had at the moment when she said, "Keep this with you always, as it will protect you." I couldn't take my eyes off of it for the longest time. My head was spinning. I thought about the strange sense of peace that I experienced as the explosions left me untouched. It was a miracle. I closed my hand and thanked God. The little medallion did just what she said it would do. Peace fell over me now as my tired and battered body lay quietly on that cot. I closed my hand and held the little medallion close to my heart and fell into deep sleep.

I was told that the first nineteen letters arrived at home all at the same time. It had been weeks since the tragic fate of the USS Bismarck Sea. Till that moment they had no way of knowing if I was dead or alive. Now it was a celebration. "Tell Danny to hang in there," I wrote, "I will be home before his birth."

Excitement ran to the highest as I walked towards her. I was amazed that she made it all the way to San Diego. The homecoming was one of the most bittersweet moments of my life. Love for her and my unborn child filled my heart but the tragedy of the war was still freshly imprinted in my mind. Still, I was home. The drive back to Los Angeles seemed endless. I was given a thirty-day leave to see my family. It was not much but it was sure heaven to us. The US Navy still owned me and I would be returning to duty. We spoke of the miracle that happened on the sea that night. We looked at each other in utter amazement. I held the little medallion in my hand. It seemed none the worse for wear. I wondered what that nun would say if she knew what happened. One day, we decided, we would find her and share with her the events of that night. But for now I was not only thankful for my life, but also for a new life, as our baby was just about to enter the world.

One week after the miracle homecoming we welcomed another miracle into our lives, the birth of our third child. It was Sunday, April 8, 1945 at the naval hospital in Long Beach, California. Only Danny turned out to be Annie.

It was the third or fourth week since her birth. "The Navy will have my duty papers ready anytime now," I said. We discussed future plans and decided Annie would be baptized before the Navy reclaimed her daddy. We made arrangements at the St. Vibiana's Catholic Church for her baptism. It was a small ceremony - only the two of us, our Annie and her future Godmother attended. We walked into the big old church and went forward into the vestibule. I noticed the four people sitting quietly in the back of the church as we entered but never gave it a second thought. I was wearing my best dress Navy uniform for the occasion. The baptism was over quickly but we stayed for a good while afterwards talking to the priest. He wanted to hear more about the war, especially the miracles that seem to revolve around the little medallion. We then bid our goodbyes and the priest began to walk with us to the door. Suddenly the four people stood up and walked in our direction. "Excuse us, sir. May we please have a word with you?"

"Sure," I responded. The four of them seemed distraught and anxious as the younger of the two men spoke. "We noticed that you were wearing a Navy uniform and we began to discuss the possibility that you might be able to help us with some information."

"If I can," I responded.

"Some weeks ago we received word from the United States Government that our son/grandson was missing in action while serving his country in the battle over Iwo Jima. We find it so difficult to live not knowing if he is dead or alive. It is painful to think that he may be a prisoner somewhere enduring the evils and tortures of the enemy. We pray for his safe return and for strength to endure whatever he is going through. But if he is dead, we want to begin to mourn him and bury him in our hearts. The not knowing is more painful than you can ever imagine. We found it more and more difficult to stay at home and do nothing so we decided to travel to San Diego."

"We know that it is the entry place for the men coming back home. We have spent days of frustration and sadness in San Diego as no one could give us any information. We know nothing more now than we did the day we received the news. We traveled hundreds of miles to come here and sadly we decided it was time to go home. We began our journey back but continued to pray for a miracle. Suddenly we were directed to Los Angeles, and then to this church where we have been sitting for the longest time. Can you imagine our excitement when you walked into the church with your new baby, wearing that uniform?"

"There were a lot of men lost in the battle over Iwo Jima; the chances of my knowing anything are so remote. There were so many vessels out there fighting this battle and there were thousands of men. Even on my own vessel there were hundreds of men. I didn't know most of them. I wouldn't recognize them if I passed them on the street. Was he in the Navy?" The man was tearful but hopeful for the miracle that they sought.

With deep emotions he answered. "Yes, he was in the Navy, aboard the USS Bismarck Sea."

Not a sound could be heard for what seemed an eternity. The silence seemed to mirror the silence that was experienced just a few short months before on Christmas Eve aboard the vessel that now lay deep in a watery grave. In my own silence I could once again hear a bell ringing far off in the distance. How I wished I could have described those few moments then and now. The words of a prayer that touched the hearts of so many shipmates bringing them to tears asking God to bring peace and comfort to loved ones struggling with worry and concern at home were now the final blessing given to the family of the man who offered them to all of us. "An act of Devine Intervention," said the priest as the man bowed his head and said, "He was the Chaplain."

To honor all those aboard the USS Bismarck Sea CVE-95, known as the "Busy Bee." Of her 943 men two-thirds would survive to tell the story thanks to the heroic efforts of Captain Burroughs and the crew of the Destroyer Edmonds who risked their lives to save them. The church of baptism was Saint Vibiana's Catholic Church on LaBrea near Wilshire Blvd, Los Angeles, Ca. April/May 1945.

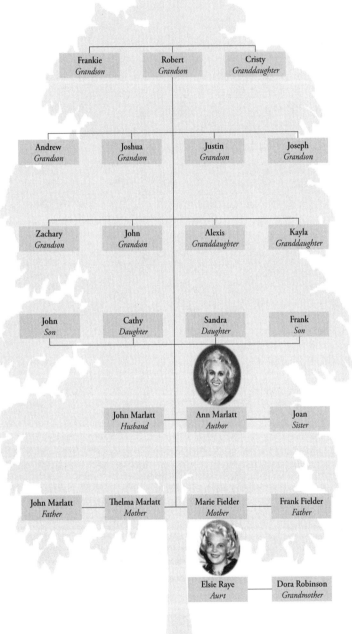

Frankie	Robert	Cristy
Grandson	*Grandson*	*Granddaughter*

Andrew	Joshua	Justin	Joseph
Grandson	*Grandson*	*Grandson*	*Grandson*

Zachary	John	Alexis	Kayla
Grandson	*Grandson*	*Granddaughter*	*Granddaughter*

John	Cathy	Sandra	Frank
Son	*Daughter*	*Daughter*	*Son*

John Marlatt	Ann Marlatt	Joan
Husband	*Author*	*Sister*

John Marlatt	Thelma Marlatt	Marie Fielder	Frank Fielder
Father	*Mother*	*Mother*	*Father*

Elsie Raye	Dora Robinson
Aurt	*Grandmother*

Story Two

Is there a purpose in each of our lives that we are born to accomplish? Is there a time frame to each lifetime? Some people say that death comes when it comes and others will argue that it comes when it is your destined time to die. Just ask Elsie. She will gladly give you her opinion after this happened to her on my birthday in the 1950's.

It was the 8th of April. I was strangely calm as I lay there listening to the conversation between my family members. Now in a coma I was suddenly out of pain but could hear everything going on around me. I looked around the room to see my husband, my mother, father and other family members gathered in a group on the left side of my bed, and a very large man with big hands standing in the shadows far behind them. I couldn't quite make out who it might be. I thought that I was moving but in actuality my body was lying perfectly still from the coma. The doctors arrived just as my father turned to leave the room. They told him that he shouldn't leave and encouraged all of them to stay. The news was not good and they were all advised to say their last goodbyes to me. My father grew angry with one of my doctors and began yelling. "I'm a doctor, not God," she responded back to him. I heard them say that they would be pulling the sheet up over my head in just a few moments.

A calm serenity now filled my whole being as I thought about what they had said. The events of the past few weeks played out in my head one last time as I lie there, expecting each breathe to be my last. It was a deep sense of peace and acceptance I was now feeling. I was ready to die

It was three months earlier, on the 9th of January that all this had begun. I had been plagued with bowel adhesions from a ruptured appendix that occurred in my youth. I had problems over the years and more than one surgery to release the adhesions but recently, despite my inability to keep anything down, my doctors said that they could find nothing wrong. For days I lay in my bed at home, unable to take anything by mouth. As my condition grew steadily worse, the pain was becoming unbearable. A chiropractor friend coming to wish my mom happy birthday and check on me found me in such distress that he phoned my doctor. My doctor came to the house, took one look at my swollen belly, put me in his car and raced me to the hospital. Over the next three months, one bowel obstruction after another sent me back to the operating room three times to remove more and more colon, but despite all the intervention, the problem persisted. I became too weak and no longer able to continue to fight to stay alive. I accepted my fate and was ready to go.

I was positioned on my back and suddenly became aware of a very bright light that appeared to the right of my bed. I turned my head toward the light and standing beside me was Jesus. The light was from him and around him. The light was intense but I could still see him very clearly. He was such a big man with very large hands. I will never forget those hands. It would be many years later when I would realize that it was he standing in the shadows behind my family that day. It was the most wonderful thing that I had ever experienced. Death was coming so easily, so peacefully. I was not afraid and it felt wonderful to know I was going home. I reached out my right hand to take his, but to my surprise he said, "Do not touch me. I have not come for you. It is not your time." I looked deeply into his eyes and face with wonder. I didn't want this to end; I didn't want him to leave me. The light with Jesus moved slowly down towards the foot of my bed, stopping there as if for one final reassurance and then began to just fade away.

I can't say how much time had passed; it could have been five minutes or five hours before I became aware of my surroundings. I could once again hear the voices in the room and somehow found the strength to turn to my side. It was then I heard one of the doctors yell out that I was moving. The doctors praised God, commenting about miracles as they began to examine me.

Shortly thereafter I was fully awake and aware of what was going on. I had tubes and lines everywhere but most disturbing was that darn hose they had shoved up my backside. Well that has to go, I thought to myself, and pulled the thing out.

In just a few days I was well on my way to recovery and home from the three-month ordeal but it wouldn't be the last of that terrible experience. Over the next few months I had many admissions to the hospital to deal with the problems that developed with my leg. A nurse mistakenly injected a medicine directly into the vein in my leg rather than into the IV fluid bottle. My leg became filled with large black sores that finally progressed to gangrene. On my last admission, the doctors called a specialist. When all other treatment failed he scheduled me for yet another surgery - an amputation. I was furious with all of them and decided after all that had happened and all that I had been through, if it was now my time, I was going to die with my leg on. I told my husband to bring the wheel chair and he took me home.

It has been fifty years since those events took place. I can promise you that over the years I have not been a stranger to many critical medical situations that should have taken my life, but I assure you I am still alive and kicking. Kicking with the leg that was scheduled for amputation.

For many years of my youth I would hear the worry and concern of my fathers family over the well being of my Aunt Elsie. There were many medical emergencies that could have and possibly should have taken her life but we would see one miracle after another where her life was concerned. At the family gatherings Elsie would laugh as the entire group agreed that Elsie would probably out live them all. As of this writing, Elsie is indeed the last surviving member of my father's family.

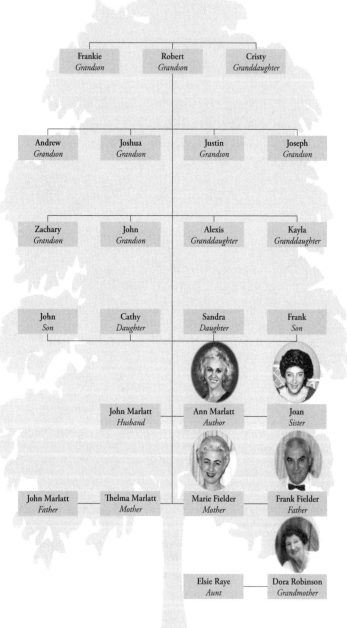

Frankie	Robert	Cristy
Grandson	*Grandson*	*Granddaughter*

Andrew	Joshua	Justin	Joseph
Grandson	*Grandson*	*Grandson*	*Grandson*

Zachary	John	Alexis	Kayla
Grandson	*Grandson*	*Granddaughter*	*Granddaughter*

John	Cathy	Sandra	Frank
Son	*Daughter*	*Daughter*	*Son*

John Marlatt	Ann Marlatt	Joan
Husband	*Author*	*Sister*

John Marlatt	Thelma Marlatt	Marie Fielder	Frank Fielder
Father	*Mother*	*Mother*	*Father*

Elsie Raye	Dora Robinson
Aunt	*Grandmother*

Story Three

We all experience moments in our lives that we believe to be purely coincidence. You had been thinking of an old friend and suddenly the phone rings and it's him. But suppose nothing in life is by chance, and there is no such thing as a coincidence. What if everything in life is all part of fate and destiny? This story will surely make you wonder.

Mom hung up the phone. "It was Emma," she told dad. "Her brother is visiting and she is bringing him over to meet with us about the music lessons for Ann. I just couldn't be rude or hurt her feelings by putting her off again. She knows we are searching for Ed, but she just won't take no for an answer."

"Well, we have done everything we can to discourage her," said Dad. "If it means that much to her, let's just meet her brother. It doesn't change anything, but it will finally put a stop to her persistence."

It was a wonderful new neighborhood and we had great new neighbors. Emma was one of them. Mom and Dad had just recently finished their dream house and we were settling in to life in this new city. I found that I had a talent for music when my little sister Joan and I had taken dancing and singing lessons a few years back. Besides coming to watch their talented daughters perform like starlets, Mom and Dad also became fans of the young man who was the accompanist at the dance studio. He was a music student working his way through college. He shared his dreams and ambitions with my parents and they were very taken with him. They loved to listen to him play, and he related so wonderfully to the children. "If any of our kids should ever decide they want private lessons, he will be the one that will teach them." So, that was it! Ed was marked as my music teacher of the future. Of course, he agreed to take on the responsibility of educating the next brilliant musically-gifted divas of the world.

The years passed and I found myself wanting to follow that dream of music. I was a young teenager now and I didn't even remember who Ed was. Mom and Dad, on the other hand, never forgot him or the promise that they made to seek him out. We had moved twice to two different cities and the phone number that they had for Ed was lost years before. They never knew where Ed lived and they didn't even know his last name but they were determined to find him. Why they were so obsessed with this was beyond me. They were going to find him one way or another. They were like hound dogs sniffing out one dead-end lead after another. They found the old music studio owner from years before but she had no clue where Ed was. Even our new neighbors were offering opinions and suggestions now. Finding Ed seemed to be the major preoccupation of everyone except for Emma. "I think you should give up this search and just meet my brother," she said. "He just happens to be the head music teacher at one of the local high schools and teaches private lessons on the side."

Well now you have it, my parents were totally obsessed with finding Ed, and Emma was obsessed with getting her brother into the house. I just wanted voice lessons, and I sure couldn't understand why they were all acting like crazy people over a music teacher that I didn't even remember. None of them were going to back down. The battle line was drawn. Will her brother become my new music teacher? Would they continue the search for the old music teacher? I really thought this was pretty funny. Yeah, destiny was calling. I laughed.

The silence was almost deafening as Emma and her brother walked in. My parents stood still. Not a word was spoken for an uncomfortably long time. For Mom and Dad, and one surprised music teacher, this truly was fate. For an astounded neighbor, it was totally unbelievable. For me, it was my new music teacher, Or was it the old music teacher? Or was it the new old music teacher? Either way, my parents just said, "Hello, Ed. We have been searching for you."

The excitement ran high. They all agreed that this was an incredible coincidence. They laughed and talked about old times and by next Saturday morning, I had a new music teacher. Or is it an old music teacher? Ed turned to the large birdcage in the corner of the living room and said he couldn't help but notice the little bird singing away during our visit. "His name is Pretty Boy!"

The months passed. It was a pretty typical Saturday morning and I was expecting Ed for my lesson. Ed came in, turned and walked straight to the living room. He looked over by the piano and said, "Well, he seems his old chipper self today!"

"Hum. Well good morning to you, too, Ed," I chuckled. "He is quite recovered from last week's hangover."

"Are you sure he is ok?" Ed inquired.

"Yes. Look, he must have heard your voice! He's waiting for you at the piano."

The two of them exchanged small talk as Grandma came into the room with their usual Saturday morning snack. "This is totally disgusting," I said jokingly. Ed laughed his usual jolly laugh as grandma set the toast and milk down on the piano for the two of them to share. It had become the pre-music lesson ritual. Nothing more could happen till they broke bread together and shared a glass of milk. I can't believe that this picture-perfect moment was my music teacher and our little blue parakeet.

"Hey, remember me?" I said laughing. "I'm the one who is supposed to be getting the lesson here. You know, we think Pretty Boy has a problem," I said in a most concerned voice. With that, Ed became quite concerned.

"What's wrong with him?"

"I think he is an alcoholic."

Ed began to laugh.

"I can't believe we are having this conversation," I said. "Pretty Boy has a taste for alcohol, especially the hard stuff." He usually had free reign of the house and his cage was rarely locked. The exception was those times when he could get hurt or when he would be in danger. Everyone loved him because he was so social. When alcohol was served he would be found hiding behind the sofa or a chair waiting for someone to put his or her glass down so he could jump up on the glass and help himself.

That particular night, we overlooked locking him up and Pretty boy really tied one on. My father was having a business-type cocktail party and Pretty Boy went totally unnoticed till he came out from under the sofa staggering across the floor. He tried to sing and talk but his language was pretty slurred. He flapped and flapped his wings but he never was able to get off the ground. He seemed so happy. I don't know, can you say that about a parakeet? We picked him up and put him in his cage on his favorite perch, but in a few moments, he passed out. We were in a panic because we thought he was dead but, thank goodness, he was only dead drunk. The next day, he moaned and just wouldn't sing his usual songs so we made the assumption that Pretty Boy had a hangover.

"Well, finally," I said, "the breakfast is over and the voice lesson can begin." Ed played the piano, I sang and Pretty Boy ran up and down the piano singing along. When the music stopped, Pretty Boy would stop, too. It was a most unusual sight. I knew in a few short months that Ed was not there to give me a voice lesson; he just wanted to play with that bird.

Ed came to see the bird more and more often. He would stop by on his way to visit with Emma but somehow just never got over there. I once overheard him saying something about divorce. She was totally angry because he began to buy one parakeet after another; he wanted so much to have a Pretty Boy of his own. His house became so full of birds that his wife gave him an ultimatum: "It's the birds or me!" He began slowly giving the birds away and one day sadly admitted that Pretty Boy was a once-in-a-lifetime friend. Ed loved that bird so much. "Pretty Boy," he'd playfully promise, "I'm going to take you home with me one day."

Pretty Boy was a one-of-a-kind little bird, a family treasure. He was never a purchase from a pet store. He was not given to us by a friend. It was actually he who found and adopted our family, not the other way round.

It was a typical summer day. The small back yard was crowded with all the neighborhood kids. The boys were having a serious game of baseball, which our dog was constantly interfering with. From out of nowhere it seemed, this little blue parakeet just flew in and decided to stay. He landed on the dog's head, and then flew to my brother. We knew the dog had only one thought: mid-afternoon snack. We ran about chasing the dog and trying to rescue the bird. Strangely, it just didn't seem to want to leave. My brother finally had him in his hand and took him in the house to where my grandmother was preparing dinner. Four little faces confronted Grandma with, "Please, can we keep him? Can we?" At first my grandmother would have no part of it but then stated, "Well, it will be up to your parents when they get home." By that night we had a cage with all the trimmings. But my parents warned, "We will put an ad in the paper. This little bird is too tame to be wild. He has to be somebody's special pet." We prayed that no one would come. We received several calls and one visit. But no one claimed him.

The weeks passed by and we all came to love that little bird. He was a constant source of entertainment for all of us. He loved playing in an eggshell and running amuck through the water at bath time and, as the train whistle blew on my brother's train set, you would find him the only passenger aboard that train playfully screeching "Low bridge! Low bridge!" as the train approached the tunnel. The weeks turned into months and the months to years. Pretty Boy was indeed a unique member of our family - a true gift from out of the blue.

It was another Saturday morning. The phone rang. "It was Ed," said my grandmother. "He's not feeling too well today and he is not coming over. He's been complaining of his stomach hurting a lot lately. Having a lot of indigestion, too." His family had been trying to get him to go see a doctor for a long while, but he was convinced that it was just indigestion. We were all very concerned because he never missed an opportunity to see

Pretty Boy. We put it aside for the time being, assuming that he must have an ulcer or something. "Yes," we all decided, "he will be ok."

But that was not what was to be. Ed's illness was more serious than anyone realized. Ed was diagnosed with cancer. He had become so ill so fast that he would not be back to teach again. It was difficult to believe that he was so filled with life such a short time ago and now was so close to death. We spoke about him and how he'd never be able to make his visits to Pretty Boy again. I wondered if Ed ever thought about Pretty Boy anymore. He was so ill now, struggling with life and death. I wondered - does a little bird have the capacity to miss a human friend? The thoughts of all the special times we shared passed through my mind: the music and laughter we all shared - how treasured I would keep these memories. I thought about the two of them together and realized that there was no earthly way that we could explain how Ed felt about that little bird, and all the coincidences that surrounded their meeting.

It was just before 7:00 a.m. when Joan started her morning chore of feeding the bird. "Good morning, Pretty Boy," she called out. Pretty Boy just did what Pretty Boy always did. He had developed quite a vocabulary over the years and he shared his usual good humor by singing and talking with her that morning. Joan walked into the kitchen, greeted the family and went about getting the bird's dishes washed and replenished with his seed and water. After a brief visit with the family she left the kitchen and headed back to the bird. A moment later we heard her screams. She stood there, looked up into our faces, and then held out her hands cradling the lifeless remains of the greatest family friend we will ever know. When she returned with his food she found him lying on the bottom of his cage. "He was just fine when I took his food containers from the cage. He was singing. He didn't act sick. What could have happened that took his life so suddenly?" she asked. Our thoughts were momentarily broken by the sound of the telephone ringing. Mom went to answer. She came back shortly and by the look on her face we knew that the news was not good. "The phone call was from Emma," Mom said. "She was calling from the hospital. Emma said that Ed's condition took a turn for the worse during the night and it is with great sadness that the family wanted to let us know that he had lost his battle with cancer. Ed died just after 7:00 a.m. this morning."

We stood like statues frozen in the moment, trying to think of some logical explanation for what we all seemed to be thinking. Could this have been some kind of wild coincidence? We discussed every possible way that Pretty Boy could have died so suddenly, except for the reason that couldn't be possible. Ed was finally able to keep his promise to his little friend. He took him home.

This story is dedicated to the memory of Ed who was the music teacher at Mark Keppel High School in San Gabriel California until his untimely death in the late 1950's. His sister Emma lived directly across the street from our home on Casa Grande in Montebello, Ca.

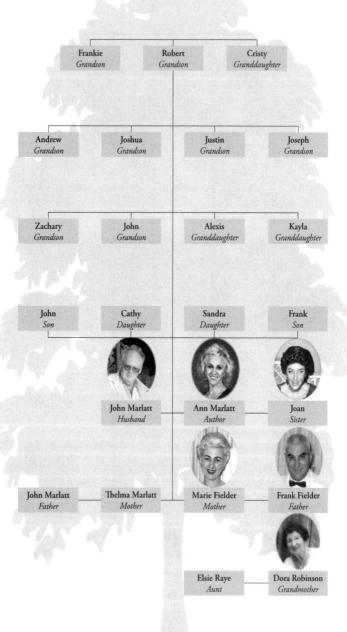

| Frankie | Robert | Cristy |
| Grandson | Grandson | Granddaughter |

| Andrew | Joshua | Justin | Joseph |
| Grandson | Grandson | Grandson | Grandson |

| Zachary | John | Alexis | Kayla |
| Grandson | Grandson | Granddaughter | Granddaughter |

| John | Cathy | Sandra | Frank |
| Son | Daughter | Daughter | Son |

| John Marlatt | Ann Marlatt | Joan |
| Husband | Author | Sister |

| John Marlatt | Thelma Marlatt | Marie Fielder | Frank Fielder |
| Father | Mother | Mother | Father |

| Elsie Raye | Dora Robinson |
| Aunt | Grandmother |

Story Four

Do you believe that parts of our lives are shaped by fate? It was the summer of my seventeenth year, a time when destiny would intersect my path and my life would change forever. The days of my youth would come to an end and my purpose driven journey would begin.

It started simply enough. My dad, a partner, and two valued employees started a new business venture. Finances were tight so I was asked to pitch in and work in the factory for the summer. Guess you could say I was the cheap help. John was there as a favor to *his* dad, who had excitedly come along from the old employer where he and my dad had met.

When I first saw John I couldn't take my eyes off of him. It wasn't just an instant physical attraction or love at first sight, it was something very different. I had this strange feeling of anger with him and I couldn't figure out why. As the days passed I began to feel a sense of relief that he had finally come into my life and yet annoyed that it took him so long to catch up with me. I was confused and quiet over the new feelings that occupied my thoughts. I became more and more attracted to John and I sensed that we were somehow destined to be together. We worked so closely over the next few months that it gave us endless time to talk, and to my surprise, he had the same feelings from the beginning about me. Before that summer would end, and before John and I ever had our first date, I told my parents that John was the man I was supposed to marry. My father was just blown away. How could I make such a ridiculous statement? My mom laughed and accepted the idea, and my grandma said she believed that meeting John was not an accident or chance. Our relationship moved very quickly and by our first date we were already planning our future.

The first time that John picked me up at home I introduced him to my grandmother, Nanny. I loved her beyond anything of this earth. It was her blessing that I was seeking most. The most loving memories of my youth were all centered on her and the music she instilled in my life. Music became my therapy, my grace, my place to hide when the world just became too much for me. As I grew up, my deepest desire was to be just like her and love just the way she taught me to love.

John and Nanny formed an instant bond. She loved his company and he loved to be with her. She told him how she worried about what would happen to me if she weren't there. She made him promise to always take good care of me. He was happy to make that promise to her. "I am happy and at peace knowing that John will take good care of you," she shared with the both of us. Then with a deep sigh added, "Now I can finally go home."

Over the next few weeks, she was the happiest I had seen her in many years. Her health was very frail but she seemed to have an inner strength and peace. She spoke frequently and freely about the visits she was now having with Grandpa and that he would soon be coming to take her home.

It was the middle of the night. My sister and I heard Nanny singing in the bathroom. We went to investigate and found her happily putting on make up, and rolling her hair in curlers. She apologized for making so much noise and waking us up. "Everything is fine," she said, "you two girls just go back to bed." Confused and a bit bewildered we went back to our room but quietly listened until we were sure that Nanny went to bed, too. I fell quickly back to sleep but Joan was too unsettled by her fears to rest. Tossing and turning for what seemed an endless time Joan, finally got up to check Nanny and hopefully put her fears to rest. Instead she found Nanny sitting on the side of her bed combing out her hair. She was wearing the nightgown and silk bed jacket that she had been saving for years.

"Please go back to bed Joan," said Nanny. "I don't want you to be here when Grandpa comes for me tonight."

Shocked beyond reason Joan replied, "You can't know that Grandpa will be here, Nanny, you just can't know." Nanny's pleading for her to leave did no good; Joan refused to go.

"It's time," Nanny softly whispered. "Grandpa is here."

Nanny looked over to Joan, smiled, whispered one last goodbye, and turned her eyes to the corner of the room. "He's waiting," she said, and with a smile on her face she reached out her hand. She told Grandpa her job on Earth was done and how much she wanted to go with him. With that, she fell back on the bed and was gone.

For the first time in my life I knew the deep and real pain of losing someone that I cherished. In the blink of an eye my life changed and the chapters of my youth closed. At the same time I realized how deeply I had fallen in love with John, and that my purpose driven journey with him had now begun.

The company started by my father Frank Fiedler Jr. and a partner was Alpha-Tafco Inc., located on Mission Rd. in Los Angeles, California . in the early 1960's.

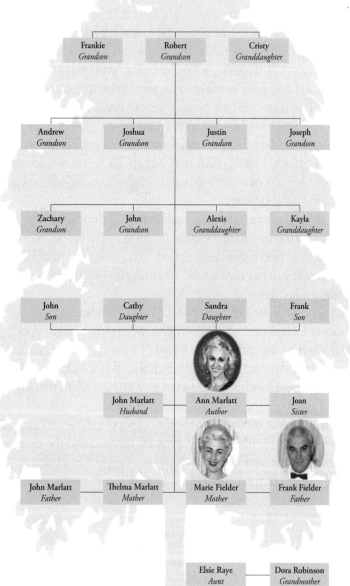

Frankie
Grandson

Robert
Grandson

Cristy
Granddaughter

Andrew
Grandson

Joshua
Grandson

Justin
Grandson

Joseph
Grandson

Zachary
Grandson

John
Grandson

Alexis
Granddaughter

Kayla
Granddaughter

John
Son

Cathy
Daughter

Sandra
Daughter

Frank
Son

John Marlatt
Husband

Ann Marlatt
Author

Joan
Sister

John Marlatt
Father

Thelma Marlatt
Mother

Marie Fielder
Mother

Frank Fielder
Father

Elsie Raye
Aunt

Dora Robinson
Grandmother

Story Five

Sometimes our first impressions of a situation can be very misleading. A policeman knocks on your door and you assume the worst, only to find out he is selling tickets to the policemen's ball. This is the story of a small, thoughtful gift that was in reality a life-changing event.

L ife had been blessed for more than twenty years since that cold and snowy day when the path of a little nun on a bus crossed the path of my Dad and Mom's. Life was good. They were blessed with four children and grandchildren were now coming into their lives, viewed as the fruits and flowers of the tree that began with the two of them. Dad started and then sold a business to a company in Indiana. He agreed to go with the company for a time to assure that the new owners would prosper. The move to Indiana made the memory of that time come flooding back to them with great intensity. They decided that it was far past time to seek out that little nun and share the joys and wonders of life that could not have been possible if it had not been for the gift of the medallion that she gave before Dad went off to war. The day was bright and beautiful as Dad and Mom headed down the highway. They laughed and joked as they joyously reconstructed that day together. Their excitement mounted as they reminisced about all the details that ended with them in that car, driven by that priest who gave them the wildest ride of their lives.

"I never thought we would get there in one piece," said Mom. "I hoped it won't take long to locate her. I wanted her to know what a powerful gift she had given to the both of us that day."

"I hoped to find that priest as well," Dad added. "I wanted to talk to him about his driving."

The front of the building had not changed a bit. "Saint Elizabeth's" it said on the very front, just the way they remembered it. They pulled into the hospital parking lot. A sense of returning to another time filled them as they looked around, surprised to find that other than a new fence around the property, the place really hadn't changed a bit in all these years.

They were excited to find out that the nun who introduced herself to them as the administrator of the hospital happened to be a nurse who had worked in the hospital for many years. She told them that she had been there since before the war, and remembered the time-frame well. Mom and Dad continue. They shared the story of the nun and the blessing of the medallion that she had given to Dad, and explained that their interest that day was in finding the nun. They described every detail that they could remember of her and the priest. They described the mood in the car as she handed the medallion to Dad and told him to keep it with him - that it would protect him and his family would always be blessed. The administrator listened intently as they continued to share stories of the strange and wondrous miracles in their lives that seemed to center around this little medallion. She was quiet and dignified, and offered no comments at the moment but instead excused herself to go to the record archives and check on records that were actually still available these many years later. Upon her return, Dad took the medallion from his wallet and showed it to her. She took it in her hand and quietly looked it over before she began to speak.

"The time that has passed since the blessing was given to you has not been long enough to erase the memory I have of the events that took place in this hospital. Still, I felt it was necessary to leave no stone unturned before I addressed your request. A surgery done in this facility on a dignitary of the church is something that I would never forget. I can now assure you that we never did any kind of surgery on a Catholic Dignitary at this facility. We have our own staff. We would never have needed to call in an outside nurse to assist. I cannot even imagine how she could fly here from Europe in those days. It was the 40's and it was wartime. Why would she need to be on a bus if there was a priest to escort her in the first place?" She paused and gently smiled as she handed the medallion back.

Her voice was soft and gentle as she again began to speak. "What you experienced that day is what we in the church call a miracle of Devine Intervention. How blessed you are indeed to have received such a gift from God. I believe your nun and the priest were sent to you to protect and watch over you and, yes, even save you for reasons that you may never know. They were heavenly beings, we call them ANGELS."

The hospital where this story took place is the "Saint Elizabeth Hospital" in Lafayette, Indiana. This was in the middle to late 1960's.

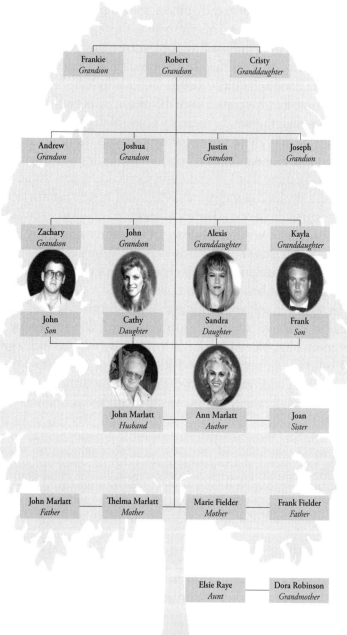

Frankie	Robert	Cristy
Grandson	*Grandson*	*Granddaughter*

Andrew	Joshua	Justin	Joseph
Grandson	*Grandson*	*Grandson*	*Grandson*

Zachary	John	Alexis	Kayla
Grandson	*Grandson*	*Granddaughter*	*Granddaughter*

John	Cathy	Sandra	Frank
Son	*Daughter*	*Daughter*	*Son*

John Marlatt	Ann Marlatt	Joan
Husband	*Author*	*Sister*

John Marlatt	Thelma Marlatt	Marie Fielder	Frank Fielder
Father	*Mother*	*Mother*	*Father*

Elsie Raye	Dora Robinson
Aunt	*Grandmother*

Story Six

There are times in each of our lives when it seems that nothing makes sense. The dreams and plans that you set out to accomplish look nothing like the reality of your life. You feel frustrated, angry and out of control. You pray but you begin to wonder if God hears you or if He is even listening. You may question your faith, or worse, you wonder if God really does exist.

John and I married in the 1960's. We wanted our life together to be a more traditional kind of partnership. I was a stay at home wife and mother, and I loved taking care of my husband and children. I was truly happy with my place in life. But something constantly invaded my peace of mind. John was having a multitude of health issues. It seemed like nothing much to be concerned about in the beginning, like frequent bouts of the flu that left him tired. Unthinkable scenarios began to filter into my head. I felt as though something or someone was always whispering a warning in my ear. What if I was suddenly without him, how could I raise our family alone? The thoughts terrified me. I tried to convince myself that he would be well soon, but I could never shake the feelings.

Going back to enroll in college was a real nightmare. It flooded me with emotions. I didn't want my life to change. I have never felt so out of place in my life. I went to the bathroom and cried. I wanted to be home for my family. I started to run away from campus when that nagging thought about the future of my children returned to me. I stopped myself from running and turned back. I opened the office door and stood staring at the woman behind the desk.

"Do you have an appointment, Ma'am?" Lord! They called me ma'am. I was feeling older by the minute. Not able to find an advisor or even a single open class for the next semester, I wandered about the campus wondering what to do next. I ended up in the nursing department. Nursing? I thought, No way. I have no desire to be a nurse, now or ever.. Besides, I rationalized, looking at the information on the bulletin board; the waiting list is more than three years long. I turned to walk away, feeling an instant sense of relief.

"Interested in becoming a nurse?" A woman spoke out from behind me. I thought to myself, Not in this lifetime. But not wanting to be rude, I told her I knew how impossible it was to get into any nursing program, or any classes for that matter at that late date, so I would come back next semester.

"Give me your name and number," she said. "I am thinking about starting a nursing assistant class. If I can get enough interest I will call you." Why did I ever leave my name? I drove home glad that I would be back in my own familiar territory. This is where I belong, I thought. I would have many years to decide which way my life should go once my children are grown. I just didn't want to consider any other alternatives.

The phone call came about a week later. A white uniform, meeting place and a time, and my life would never be the same. Over the years my career blossomed. A few weeks after the start of my class, I was hired by the hospital. I didn't know how to say no when they offered me a job. Suddenly short-handed and needing someone to temporarily fill in, I agreed. The job would be short-lived because the facility only hired licensed nurses, or so I thought. Fate came into play as that job turned into a nursing career. When I looked back over the years, it was so obvious that this is where I was meant to be. There was no coincidence. It was my destiny to be a nurse in that little hospital.

It was a very difficult time for me. I continued to struggle over the issues with my family. Problems were arising at home. I felt angry and frustrated. I should be home with my children, not here in pediatrics taking care of other children. I doubted my whole life. Had I convinced myself that it was God's intervention that put me in this small barrio hospital? Fate? Destiny? Or a feeble attempt to justify why I left my children? Had I accepted my place with such little regard for my own family? Is this really God's will or just my own agenda? I was so confused. I remember how I struggled to become an RN. It's not something I wanted to do, life just pulled me along this path. It took all the strength I had inside to get up in the morning, leave the house and my children and go to the hospital. But when I got to the pediatric floor the needs of those children and their families just seemed to occupy my soul. How could I have been so sure that God put me here? My children need me. What about my needs as a mother? This is definitely not the way I planned *my* life.

Things were not easy at home. My husband's health problems continued to escalate. No matter how hopeful I was that he would recover, it never happened. What once was so clear just caused me pain and confusion. I could share my thoughts and fears with no one. I felt the pressure breaking me. The days turned into weeks, then months. I couldn't stop crying. No one knew, not even my husband, of the struggle that was going on inside of me. "No more!" I yelled out. I am ready to hear the truth. "Please God, give me a sign that I am following what I believed was your will and not my own agenda."

The television channel was tuned to an evangelist ministry program. Somehow through my tears, the words fell onto my ears. My eyes glanced to a small plaque sitting at the table edge beside me. I read it over and over. Let go and let God. Let go and let God. I screamed out in my heart, I can't let go and let God! I am afraid to let go. I don't know if I believe you are really there. My world is falling down around me and I can't let go. On the television, a lady was speaking. "There is a woman crying out for answers. I am confused about the message. I am just going to tell you to let go and let God." Over and over she repeated the message, let go and let God. "Someone," she said, "knows what this means."

It was enough to bring me to my senses. I was smiling now; in fact, I was laughing my head off, totally amused that God would give me some kind of message through a television evangelist. Well, at least I wasn't crying any more. Ok God, here's the thing. You are going to have to hit me with a 2x4 to make me believe any message you send me. I want the real truth. Until then, I will just keep doing what I have always done: my best at whatever I am doing.

It was an exhausting day from the moment I walked in. In the early afternoon the phone rang with two more admissions. The first little boy had a ruptured appendix. He was very ill and needed to be readied for surgery immediately. There were IV lines to start and medications to give. His temperature was over 107 degrees. The climate on the floor was hurried but instinct and skills took over. The fever was a major concern. It would have to be controlled before we could safely take him to surgery. The parents were frantic, crying with disbelief. Their little boy was in real danger of losing his life. We worked as quickly as we could to bring the fever down, and got medications on board to prevent a tragedy from happening. I worked with the child and the parents to help make the situation as tolerable as possible. I tried to give them hope and reassurance that God would see them through, and the knowledge that the physician was a good man to have in their corner.

Suddenly, as I readied the little boy for surgery, a second little boy came to the floor. He was having a seizure. Oh God, I prayed, please be with us all and work through me to help these children. There was another IV line to start and more medications to give. The pediatrician walked into the room and stayed with the second child as I worked between the two boys. His temperature was over 107degrees! How can this be, I asked silently. I had never seen two children with fevers of this intensity and both at the same time. I was fearful for both children and their families. The second child had an infection around his brain. We worked quickly to get his seizures and his fever under control. I tried to comfort his parents. His father seemed unusually calm, the mother was crying. He spoke very little English and she spoke none. I continued to pray that God would guide my hands to help these children and the parents through this terrible time. Though the hours passed slowly for the parents, the hours for me passed quickly. By the end of my shift, the immediate danger with both boys was successfully over. I breathed a sigh of relief. Thank you, Father, for my nursing skills; thank you for using me this day, I prayed. I left the floor for home.

I opened my eyes to another day still feeling exhausted from the one before. It was all I could do to pull myself up out of that bed and get to work. It was quiet when I reached the pediatric unit. I sat down, got the reports, and went to see how my little guys were doing. The first child did very well in surgery. His appendix was ruptured but he was responding nicely to treatment. I approached my little guy in a manner that would ease his fears and finished my examination. From behind me I felt his mother gently touched my shoulder. I turned towards her. She had tears in her eyes and began to speak. "It must be the most wonderful thing in the world for you to know that you are where God wants you to be in life." I looked puzzled at her gentle and thankful face and she continued. "We all go through life and not ten percent of us will ever truly know that we are really doing what we were put on this earth to do. You have that knowledge and that satisfaction. You know that God put you here. He gave you the skills to be more than an excellent nurse. You have no idea what you have done for us as parents. Your spirit shines. We are all so grateful that God sent you to this little hospital to care for all of us. You kept my child from becoming frightened, and did the same for us as parents. I will never know how to thank you so I will just thank God because I know he put you here."

I thanked her and turned to walk away but standing there at the door way was the father of the other young boy. With his broken English he said, "You do not remember me?" He smiled and gave me a moment to think. I did recognize him from somewhere but I could not recall. In his very broken English and with the assistance of an interpreter he said "Two years ago my back got broke at work and you took care of me. I never forget you because you were so nice and gentle. My son got very sick and I didn't know what to do. I was so scared that he would die. I put my family in the car and drove. I didn't know where to go. I ended up outside. Then Jesus came to me. He told me not to be afraid because HE was with my son. He told me to take my son inside and told me that you would be there to take care of my son and my son will be okay. Did you not see how calm I was? I smiled at you when I saw you because I was told you would be there. I knew it would be ok when I saw you. I was not afraid anymore. I knew you would take care of my son and my family." We exchanged brief conversation as he thanked me for doing what God put me there to do. I began to weep. I walked past him through the door into the hallway and to my astonishment was confronted with other parents of other children on the unit. I stood there in absolute amazement as they began to speak.

"We were all talking about you last night, Ann. We all started telling each other about our times with you. We all became so grateful to God that we formed a prayer circle in the hall to ask God to bless you. We wanted to thank Him for putting you in this place for all of us. We want you to know how we all feel about you and what you have done for each of our families. We wanted God to know that we knew He put you here for all of us." I was overwhelmed by what I had heard and I thanked each one as they began to turn and go back to their children. I found my way back to the station, took a deep breath, sighed and picked up my pen to begin my charting.

Suddenly like a bolt of lightening it struck me. A little voice in my head was calling out. Well? Well? Do you get it yet? It was only then that I realized that my prayer had been answered in a most unexpected way. I remember the pen falling from my fingertips and I began to cry. "Oh God," I said. "Was this a 2x4 or a whole building falling in on me?" I left the station and found a place to be alone. I cried and cried until I couldn't cry anymore. All the months of struggling with the guilt of leaving my family was melting into tears of gratitude. Still, the other part of me that longed to be home with my family was grieving for a time that would never return. It was never my destiny to be a stay at home wife and mom. Another fate was planned for me long before. I grieved for that loss in my life, too. That day God and I had the most wonderful talk. I knew He had planned for me to care for many children, not just my own, but a world of children. My mind wandered over my situation at work and the many times my bosses would call me Mother Theresa and tell me I couldn't save all the kids in the world. Well maybe not, I thought, but somehow maybe I could make a little difference here. I thanked Him for the blessing of my family and for the gift of my children. They were the most beautiful and important things in my life.

"God, I don't understand why you put me here to care for all of these children, but at least now I do know that this is your will. So now, I need to give you custody of mine. I trust you with all my heart. I trust that you will always be with my children especially in those times when I cannot be there for them." The sound of an IV pump ringing brought me back to the day at hand. I smiled knowing that the child was told that the ringing pump was their very own special R2D2 robot and would send me a message to come and check on things. They were excited when the alarm went off. It made them feel special.

To this day, I am aware that my children are in His wonderful hands. It has not kept them from experiencing some enormous challenges in life, and I have had many moments where I wished things could have been different. That day left me with no doubt for the rest of my life. God, do you really even hear me...are you really there? Yes, prayer is always answered even if it's not what you want to hear.

This was on the pediatric unit at the "Greater El Monte Community Hospital" located on Santa Anita Ave. in So. El Monte, California. It was here that I spent a good many years of my nursing career in many capacities, including the supervisor of nursing. I helped open this pediatric unit and helped to start the suspected child abuse and neglect team that expanded into the community with the assistance of law enforcement and other community agencies that made this unit a shinning example of a community pulling together, and many wonderful pediatricians who were the mentors of many nurses.

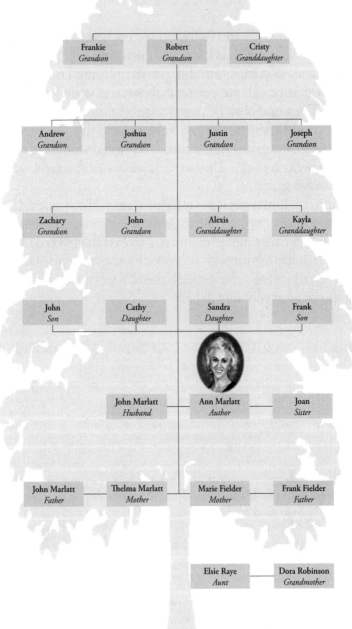

Frankie
Grandson

Robert
Grandson

Cristy
Granddaughter

Andrew
Grandson

Joshua
Grandson

Justin
Grandson

Joseph
Grandson

Zachary
Grandson

John
Grandson

Alexis
Granddaughter

Kayla
Granddaughter

John
Son

Cathy
Daughter

Sandra
Daughter

Frank
Son

John Marlatt
Husband

Ann Marlatt
Author

Joan
Sister

John Marlatt
Father

Thelma Marlatt
Mother

Marie Fielder
Mother

Frank Fielder
Father

Elsie Raye
Aunt

Dora Robinson
Grandmother

Story Seven

Have you ever had a feeling so strong that it wouldn't leave you alone? You try to convince yourself that the feeling is just your imagination running away with you. You try to ignore it but it keeps getting stronger until you finally decide to check it out even at the risk of looking foolish. This was one of those situations.

The freeway had been moving really fast that morning. I was going at least 70 mph. I was driving a little front wheel Champ. Not a really big or safe car, but it got me to where I was going and was wonderful on gas. I was really feeling rather badly about having to go to work on my birthday, but it was what I had to do. "What is that smell?"I said to my self. "It smells like a cigar." I looked around the car and began to feel like someone or something was riding along with me. The cigar smell became so strong that I turned up the air-conditioner. I kept looking over to the passenger seat, half-expecting to see something or someone sitting there. The feeling just kept growing stronger and stronger. I had a vision in my head of white owl cigars. I remembered my grandfather smoked them for many years. Another familiar scent began to fill the car. It was the smell of my grandfather. I was moving down memory lane thinking of him. I felt really silly when I said hello and thanked him for the birthday visit. I was really rather amused. But my amusement was short-lived and suddenly replaced with a strong sense of danger. I tried to shake the feeling but it just got more intense. "This suddenly doesn't feel much like a social call," I spoke out. Maybe this is a warning.

I checked all the gauges and even moved the car to one side and then the other to allow the tires to hit on the raised lane bumps in the road. I knew that if a tire was getting low it would make a different sound and have a different feel when going over those bumps. I could find nothing to be alarmed about and kept driving. The nagging feeling would not leave me and in fact, was growing stronger by the moment. The harder I tried to ignore it the more unsettled I was becoming. I saw the next off ramp coming up quickly. I caved in to the feeling. "OK!" I yelled out loud. "I will get off the freeway and see if I can find something wrong." I swerved my car quickly across the four lanes of traffic to the off ramp and began to decrease my speed. I was nearly to the red light when I heard a thump. I was only going about five to ten miles an hour and moving up hill but for a split second I lost control of the steering. I rolled to a stop and got out of the car. I saw what was left of my front tire a few yards behind my car. The steel belt detached from the entire tire. There was absolutely nothing left of that tire. I stood there frozen thinking about what just happened. I got back into the car to wait for help to arrive. I was thankful that I was waiting for a tow truck and not an ambulance to take me to the nearest hospital, which was ironically where I was headed in the first place. "Thanks, Grandpa, this is indeed a very blessed birthday."

I was traveling west on the Pomona (60) freeway at the Azusa Exit off ramp. City of Industry, California. Tire company was Winston tire which was located on Colima Road in Rowland Heights, California.

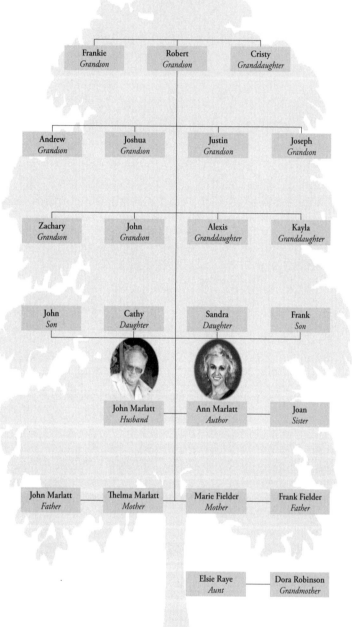

Frankie	Robert	Cristy
Grandson	Grandson	Granddaughter

Andrew	Joshua	Justin	Joseph
Grandson	Grandson	Grandson	Grandson

Zachary	John	Alexis	Kayla
Grandson	Grandson	Granddaughter	Granddaughter

John	Cathy	Sandra	Frank
Son	Daughter	Daughter	Son

John Marlatt	Ann Marlatt	Joan
Husband	Author	Sister

John Marlatt	Thelma Marlatt	Marie Fielder	Frank Fielder
Father	Mother	Mother	Father

Elsie Raye	Dora Robinson
Aunt	Grandmother

Story Eight

Extraordinary things can happen to ordinary people, and when they do, your life is changed forever. This is one that changed my life.

It was a very bright summer's day on that 4th of July morning. I stretched and thought about what the day would bring. Not much celebrating for John and I today since I had to work later that evening, and John was still recuperating from surgery. Tomorrow is John's birthday. Maybe we could do something special to celebrate his birthday on the weekend. "Hmm," I thought, "that would be fun for all of us. I know how John loves to have family around." I turned to say good morning and noticed that John was having problems. It was difficult for him to breathe. He was complaining of shoulder and neck pain; he just didn't look well. "Oh no," I gasped, "not something else wrong. Please God, not again." His condition grew steadily worse until I had to call 911.

The last thing that we ever expected was the news from the emergency room physician that John had a bad heart. For years we would make comments about all the medical emergencies he had to deal with but we always were reassured that things would be ok since he never seemed to have any signs of heart disease. Now it appears that John had a hidden heart condition. The doctor who did the angiogram said that John's heart condition was so advanced that it was too late for angioplasty. He would need, at the very least, a bypass surgery immediately. The surgeon arrived for his examination and felt that John was too unstable for surgery; it would have to wait until he was stronger. Unable to find a replacement, I went on to work. I was the administrative supervisor of nursing in another hospital. Working was very difficult that afternoon and evening. It wasn't the first time that I had to continue picking myself up and going to work while John struggled with a life and death situation without me. John had been so ill for so many years that I could not afford the luxury of just taking off work and being with him. It was very painful and not easy for me to deal with it again and again over the years.

I was exhausted by the time I reached home. Several phone calls to the hospital reassured me that John was stable and not in any life threatening danger for the time being. He would be closely observed in the cardiac care unit. I needed a hot shower, some prayer, a good cry, and a couple of hours sleep. I awakened to the ringing of the phone. I looked at the clock thinking I must have overslept but it was only an hour or so since I had gone to bed.

Fear gripped me as I answered. It was the cardiologist. I feared the worst since he was calling me at that hour. John would not be able to survive without having surgery, he told me. It is scheduled for early morning. My head was fuzzy and I was confused. "The surgeon said John was too unstable to go to surgery now," I said. The cardiologist assured me that everything was in place and it had to be now or never. He asked permission to put in some special lines. One was a balloon pump that would go into his heart from an artery in his leg. I was hesitant but he convinced me that it was the only way to save John's life. I gave my permission and got to the hospital just as the cardiologist finished inserting the balloon pump.

I held John's hand and waited by his bedside until morning turned into late afternoon. When the surgeon arrived, we spoke. "I told you that John was too unstable to go to surgery," he said. "I have not changed my mind; it's too dangerous to try to do anything to his heart now." I was confused and angry now thinking about what I allowed that cardiologist to put John through. Before I had the chance to take it all in, another surgeon walked into the room: a vascular surgeon. I heard him a few moments earlier speaking angrily to someone outside the room but I had no idea he was headed in to see John. The vascular surgeon explained that the procedure done by the cardiologist created a problem with the blood flow in John's leg. He was very kind but upset that he had not been consulted earlier. The covers were pulled back to expose a leg that was ice cold and deep blue. He looked at me with a sadness that I won't soon forget. He's been without circulation too long. I don't know if I can save his leg. I found myself signing another consent allowing the vascular surgeon to try and restore the circulation in John's leg and to amputate the leg if he could not. Sadly, I kissed him goodbye as I was sent off to a waiting room down the hall.

I was crying and angry. How could this happen? The only thing I could do was pray. God, I have spent so much time over the past 30 years with this same prayer in my heart. I should just record it and play it to you over and over. This is so difficult. I was going to beg you to save his life again.

I felt so futile in my thoughts. I felt worn down to nothing and I felt selfish, too. I don't understand why all these things keep happening to John. How would I ever get along with out him? How could I manage life with out him? I gathered all the strength I could pull from the depths inside of me. No Father, this time I will not ask you to save John's life. He has been in so much pain and through so many serious situations in the past 30 years. It just never stops! I just cannot ask you to save his life another time if it means that he will have to live with his leg removed. I thought about how difficult the past few years had been for him. I tried to envision life without him. I was terrified. How could I survive with out him? Yet, the thought of how John would have to live kept filling my whole being with pain.

God, I know that you will show me the way to survive. I want what is best now for him. Let this decision be out of my hands. Father, let him be whole or take his soul to be with you. I want only this one thing. I have to know he is with you. In all these years my own husband would never tell me how he felt about God. I cannot live on this earth not knowing. I want him to know you, find you and call on you. Maybe he has in his private moments but he has never shared this with me. It would be the thing that I could not face in life. It is so painful to even consider that he would not be there when you called me home. The doubts will fill my life forever and I will not be able to handle this. My husband has spent many years talking about my useless need for you. He hated the way I was always looking for a church to worship. Please Father: grant me this one request. I want to know that he knows you and he will be with you.

I closed my eyes and put my head back against the wall. Suddenly there was a man standing there in my vision. It startled me; I have never experienced such a thing. I began talking to him. Who are you? I don't know your face. I was getting more and more anxious and then excited. I sat straight up in the chair. I was yelling in my head. What is going on? Is this some kind of a vision? "No, it can't be!" I said. Ordinary people like me don't have visions. I sat forward in the chair but never dared to open my eyes. I thought maybe I was asleep, but I was wide-awake. I pinched myself; I pulled my hair, anything that I could think of to make sure that this wasn't some kind of a dream. I was nearly hysterical inside my head, but stayed as still as I could. I was afraid it would all go away. God, I am truly having a vision of some kind. Who is this man? I don't recognize him. Then as if a camera zoomed back, I was able to see all of him. He turned from facing me and began walking towards my left down what seemed to be a dark poorly lit hallway. He was dressed in a long robe made of white cloth with a rope like tie around his waist. This was all happening so fast. The light! I began yelling in my head, look at the light. It was a brilliant white light, like the rays of the sun only more so and coming from *Him*. It was so bright, it was radiating from his chest. This was the first that I recognized who it could be.

"Jesus?" I said.

He stopped and turned to me again.

"Jesus, Jesus!" I cried out, or at least I thought I had cried out. I was speaking with my mind and it felt so normal to speak this way.

"It's you, Jesus, it's you!" Jesus bowed; Oh God, he bowed to me! I somehow knew I was supposed to see what was going to happen. He turned back and began to walk on again. Oh God, what is happening, I yelled in my head? As I watched, Jesus walked from the darkened tunnel area towards a light at the end. I looked past Jesus and saw he was walking towards John's hospital room. I could see John lying in the bed. I was looking at him from a distance and the light of his room started where there should have been a wall at the foot of his bed. Jesus walked into the room and straight to John's bedside. They began to speak to each other. I could see what was happening but I could not hear their conversation. Jesus reached down and touched John's chest with both of his hands. They spoke again. He reached down and touched John's legs starting at his hips and running his hands to John's knees. I knew I wasn't asleep. I knew this was real and I was supposed to see this.

Suddenly Jesus and John were standing in front of me. Jesus had his arm around John's shoulder and they were both looking straight into my eyes. The depth of his eyes is just beyond description. Then Jesus spoke, *"Ann, You never have to worry. John is mine now and always will be."*

His words melted me. His presence was so commanding but his voice was so soft, so gentle, so firm and so reassuring. I looked into John's eyes and he spoke to me, too. "Ann, for the first time in twenty years I am free of pain." What I was feeling is far beyond any words I can find to express. I was in such a state of amazement and grace. I could hardly believe my own senses, but this was real. I once again looked into the brilliant eyes of Jesus with all the burning desire of a thousand questions, a million "why's" in life. I was so overwhelmed looking upon his face that the only thing I could say was "Jesus, I didn't know that you were so tall." Jesus looked into my eyes and as if a camera once again zoomed inward, I saw only his face as the vision began to fade. Then I was compelled to open my eyes.

I was awake; it was not a dream. I thought about what I had just seen. I became lost in the after-glow of what would be the most powerful moment of my life. Jesus was really with my husband. He spoke to me! Jesus is really a big man. I chuckled at my amusement, thinking about my words to him. I was giddy. I was laughing and crying both at the same time. I was dancing inside. Suddenly reality hit my senses. I began to think. I was gripped with the possibility…is John dead?

Every step was an effort as I headed down the hallway towards John's room. I didn't know what to expect. I turned the corner and walked towards his bedside. John was quiet and still as I approached him. He began to stir. He turned toward me, his eyes opened and he softly said, "Hi. I must have fallen asleep for a while." I tried to get the words out of my mouth, but John began to speak first. "Honey, for the first time in twenty years I was free of pain." I was shaking now. It was all I could do to stay on my feet. He used the exact words now that he had used a few moments earlier during the vision. I was stuttering and unable to speak. He continued, "While you were gone a man came to see me. He spoke to me and told me that I would not go to surgery for my heart today. He told me that everything would be ok, and I didn't have to worry. He touched my chest with his hands and then both of my legs, too."

I was finally able to yell out. "Jesus was with you! I saw the whole thing just as you described from the waiting room down the hall."

John said, "I didn't say it was Jesus." I laughed and cried and I held his hand knowing that the blessing that we just received would never go away. I tried so hard to tell him what I had witnessed but he took the words right out of my mouth, leaving me with no doubt then or forever. "What ever happens now, it will be in God's hands."

John was taken by ambulance to the Riverside Community Hospital, on Magnolia and 14th Street in Riverside, California from our home on Sherry Lane, Glen Avon (Riverside) California. This was July 4, 1994.

The visit from Jesus took place in the cardiac care unit of the hospital. I was in a waiting room far away from Johns' room but I saw the events like watching a remote camera only in my head. When I saw Jesus and all that happened I was pretty shaken and found it difficult to believe until John described exactly what I had seen before I could tell him what I saw. It would be days later before John would tell me that he knew it was Jesus that visited him that day. He said he was afraid that I would think he was crazy if he told me it was Jesus. We had many wonderful moments reliving that event over the next few months. We couldn't help but wonder why something so extraordinary would happen to us.

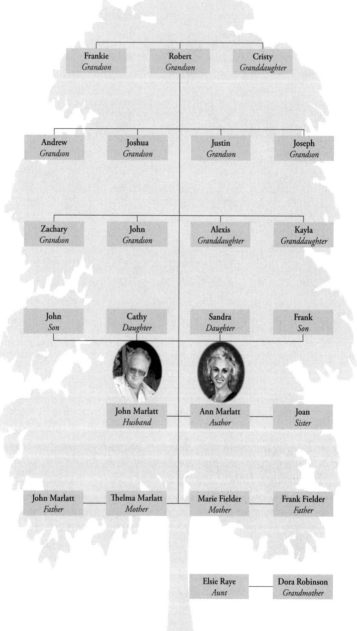

Frankie	Robert	Cristy
Grandson	*Grandson*	*Granddaughter*

Andrew	Joshua	Justin	Joseph
Grandson	*Grandson*	*Grandson*	*Grandson*

Zachary	John	Alexis	Kayla
Grandson	*Grandson*	*Granddaughter*	*Granddaughter*

John	Cathy	Sandra	Frank
Son	*Daughter*	*Daughter*	*Son*

John Marlatt	Ann Marlatt	Joan
Husband	*Author*	*Sister*

John Marlatt	Thelma Marlatt	Marie Fielder	Frank Fielder
Father	*Mother*	*Mother*	*Father*

Elsie Raye	Dora Robinson
Aunt	*Grandmother*

Story Nine

Have you ever been driven to help someone even when it interferes with your own plans? Divine intervention on your behalf can play a role even in the life of a stranger.

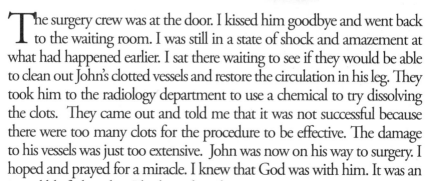

The surgery crew was at the door. I kissed him goodbye and went back to the waiting room. I was still in a state of shock and amazement at what had happened earlier. I sat there waiting to see if they would be able to clean out John's clotted vessels and restore the circulation in his leg. They took him to the radiology department to use a chemical to try dissolving the clots. They came out and told me that it was not successful because there were too many clots for the procedure to be effective. The damage to his vessels was just too extensive. John was now on his way to surgery. I hoped and prayed for a miracle. I knew that God was with him. It was an incredible feeling, but I had no idea what to expect.

I kept inventing scenarios in my mind. Maybe he was going to die. I couldn't shake the thought that he was too ill, too unstable to go to surgery, and now his heart would have to withstand another surgery. I was so overwhelmed I didn't know what to think. Maybe God was preparing me for his death. My prayer was answered and I knew it. John would be with God and I would see him again one day. But now I wondered when that would be. I would just have to wait. It seemed like forever but someone finally came to tell me that he was nearly done, and the doctor would be out to see me soon. I prepared for the worst and hoped for the best. An hour later, no one came. It was hard to stay calm. The night was endless. Finally, the doctor appeared. John has both of his legs, he told me. I began to weep. He apologized for taking so long but just as he finished the surgery using a piece of vessel from his left leg, the circulation in his left leg became occluded from that procedure. He had to repair the left side as well. "This is a miracle," the surgeon said. "We will have to see if it will last."

The first couple of days would be the most critical. The surgeon told me that he exhausted all the traditional ways of making the repairs to John's leg and nothing worked. He was preparing for the amputation and on an impulse decided to try something untraditional. "I figured we had nothing to lose by trying." He said he made small cuts into John's legs and vessels and slid catheter tubing down as far as they would go to suck out the clots. "It shouldn't have worked, but it has for now." John was alive and had both of his legs. The surgeon then excused himself and explained that he had been on his way out of town with his family for a short vacation when they called him to see John. I thanked him with all my heart for following his instinct and coming. I felt his decision to see John was not accidental.

I thanked God for his intervention in the doctor's decision to see John. I wandered back to John's room and waited for his return. I wanted to be the one to tell him that he had both of his legs. We both cried and I held his hand till he drifted off to sleep. I looked at his poor, weak body, tubes everywhere. I was amazed that his body could withstand what he had to go through the past couple of days. He was by no means out of the woods, but for now he was sleeping peacefully. I went home now, numb from the day's events. I fell into bed and cried until I fell into an exhausted sleep.

Several weeks later during our post surgical visit with the vascular surgeon in his office, John and I told the doctor about the visit we had with Jesus and how we felt that all the unusual things he (the doctor) did in the operating room that day were some how all connected and suppose to happen just the way it did. The doctor said that he was not really surprised because he had experienced other miracles in the operating room in the past. We told him that we were very grateful that he listened to the urging of the little voice in his head that made him delay his time away with his family and come to the hospital to help John. Some how I felt he really did understand.

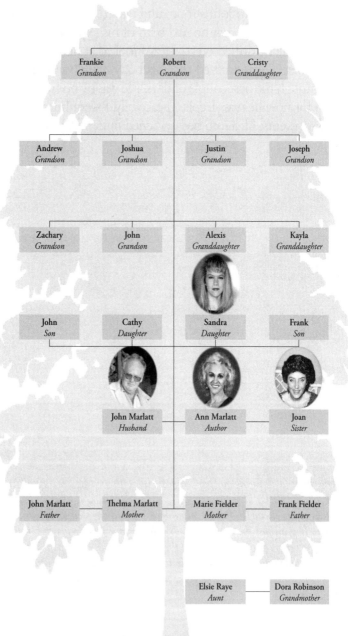

| Frankie | Robert | Cristy |
| *Grandson* | *Grandson* | *Granddaughter* |

| Andrew | Joshua | Justin | Joseph |
| *Grandson* | *Grandson* | *Grandson* | *Grandson* |

| Zachary | John | Alexis | Kayla |
| *Grandson* | *Grandson* | *Granddaughter* | *Granddaughter* |

| John | Cathy | Sandra | Frank |
| *Son* | *Daughter* | *Daughter* | *Son* |

| John Marlatt | Ann Marlatt | Joan |
| *Husband* | *Author* | *Sister* |

| John Marlatt | Thelma Marlatt | Marie Fielder | Frank Fielder |
| *Father* | *Mother* | *Mother* | *Father* |

| Elsie Raye | Dora Robinson |
| *Aunt* | *Grandmother* |

Story Ten

Even with all the Spiritual intervention surrounding our lives it had become increasingly difficult for me to give John the support and courage he needed to continue his fight for life. I felt helpless knowing that there was nothing I could do to change the way things were until this event opened my heart and mind to the power of prayer.

It had been days since the vascular surgery. John had restored pulses in his feet and the vascular surgeon, back from his vacation, was totally amazed. Pain was another issue. The lack of circulation in his right leg for so many hours left him with permanent nerve damage. The burning pain was so intense that he could not even stand a sheet to touch his leg. The toll on his body was enormous. He grew weaker and weaker needing more and more medications to keep him alive. You can't imagine the number of intravenous medications they were using to sustain his life. The stress on his already weak heart was proving to be more than he could stand. The surgeon said "the possibility of doing the bi-pass surgery was now very slim at best". "We will have to wait and see," I knew he was telling me that the crisis in John's care, made it impossible to think about that kind of surgery again.

A few days later I received a call from the cardiologist asking me to hand carry the film from the angiogram to a San Diego University Hospital for a second opinion. He gave me instructions where to find the surgeon that he had spoken to earlier and urged me to go immediately. Because there was so much friction now between the cardiologist and the surgeons, I agreed to go. My sister Joan and my daughter Sandra insisted on going with me. My own exhaustion and fear of what the doctor may tell us gave them good reason to be uncomfortable for me to face this alone. When we arrived we were told that the cardiologist had made no arrangements for the doctor to see us. I got the impression that the odds of seeing him were about zero. We waited for hours to see him. I refused to take no for an answer, so I began to wander about the facility. I learned from working in a hospital that carrying a clipboard and looking like you belong will get you a long way.

I heard the doctor's name called in the hallway. I turned and saw the man who responded, and followed him into the radiology department. I stopped him and asked for his help. He knew I was waiting for him and admitted that he had no intention of seeing me. He was very abrupt, but since I found him he would look at the film. He made a few comments about the nerve of that cardiologist expecting some kind of special treatment while he put the tape in the machine. "How does this man feel about a transplant?" he said. "That's the only thing that will save him now." My knees began to buckle and I felt Sandra brace me so I wouldn't fall. I never expected to hear those words. Maybe I just never wanted to hear what he had to say. I didn't want this man to see me fall apart. I found my voice to say thank you, and told him that I would discuss it with John. He kept the tape and told us to have the cardiologist call him.

The next few days were a blur. I was told that John was not responding to treatment, and they could not get him off the medication to sustain his blood pressure. I was told that things didn't look very good. I was barely functioning. I don't know how I made it through my shifts at work. I spoke to the cardiologists at my facility. I kept them as updated on John's condition as I could and they were trying to help me deal with this situation as best they could. I told them I wanted to get John into U.C.L.A. for treatment. I wasn't even sure if he would ever be strong enough to be transferred to another hospital. I clung to the only thread of hope I had left, prayer, and I was begging for some kind of intervention.

John began to get a little stronger. When I felt he was strong enough to talk about his heart condition, I shared the news about the transplant with him. It was a shock. He was more than overwhelmed. I convinced the both of us that we were not going to give up hope now. I don't know how he always stayed so strong over the years with all the terrible things that happened with his health. I tried to be as reassuring as I could be and told him that I would do everything in my power to get him into U.C.L.A..

When I came to visit the next day, I found John crying. He told me that the cardiologist had been in to see him. "He advised me to go to San Diego for a transplant evaluation. I told him that I was going to go to U.C.L.A. and he laughed at me. He told me that I would never get into U.C.L.A. 'You better just get that out of your head and be happy if you get accepted down in San Diego.'" The news had devastated him. I tried to comfort him but he was at the end of his rope.

I put on my best smile and told him, "Don't listen to that guy." I started to walk toward his bed when the phone rang. "Hello," I said, hoping I could end this phone call quickly and tend to John's needs.

Something in the room began to feel strange. I felt my hand with the phone drop to my side. I felt frozen to the floor. I heard it coming and looked up to the ceiling. It was a roar and a 'schoooooom.' I can't describe the sound or the feeling as it hit me. It was a bolt of white light. It was like nothing I have ever experienced in my life. I stood there shaking. The light crashed over me, through the top of my head and out my feet and the ends of my fingers. Then a sense of peace and comfort came over me as the light bathed me and soothed me. I wanted to stay in it forever. I could feel it, but I could not see anything. I just knew it was there.

I closed my eyes and suddenly I was aware that I was standing in the middle of something like a revolving carousel. I could hear voices, hundreds of voices surrounding me with conversation, but I could not make out what they were saying. I stood frozen there in the middle while everything moved around me. I listened more carefully, trying to tune into one voice at a time. It was a woman saying a prayer.. I tried to single out another voice. It was the voice of a man, another prayer. Then another prayer, and another. Oh my God, I was standing in a circle of prayer. There were hundreds, maybe thousands of prayers. I wanted to stay there, it felt so wonderful. I didn't want it to go away. "No," I said, "don't leave," as it began to fade. "Please, don't leave now."

The fading voices and the voice coming from the phone in my hand brought me slowly back to reality. "Ann, hello, are you there?" I recognized the voice and put the phone back to my ear. It was one of the cardiologists from my hospital. "I'm here Doctor D. I am sorry. I was interrupted for a moment." We spoke only briefly. I thanked her and I hung up the phone. "John," I said as I turned to him, "that was Doctor D. She has arranged for one of the world's most renowned heart surgeons to take your case. She has just finished making arrangements for transfer. Now, she wants to know. Are you ready to go to U.C.L.A.?"

The transfer to U.C.L.A. went very smoothly. John's condition was improving and he was able to be weaned off some of the medications that were sustaining his life. The news from the cardiologist and the surgeon was good. They spent many days evaluating the situation and making the preparations for the next step. The heart surgeon was confident that he could do some bi-pass surgery that would give John more circulation to his heart, and give him a better quality of life for the time being. His success rate was nearly one hundred percent. He was the best at what he did.

After the surgery, we would discuss the heart and lung transplant procedures. Arrangements were in process to put John on the transplant list. I began to gather the information about the transplant to share with John. It was only marginally successful in those days, and would allow an average life span of about two years. The treatment included spending much of his life in and out of the hospital. The conversation between us was one of the most painful in my life. I promised that I would support any decision that he made. In the meantime, John's condition was stable enough now for the surgeon to do the

78

bi-pass procedure. "It was now or never," said the cardiologist. Complicated cases that could not be done by other surgeons were the kind of cases that this surgeon performed. Everyone was so positive and reassuring, we were not afraid. I sat with him as they got him ready for the surgery, but when the time came I began to have a strange sense about the whole situation. He was wheeled from the room but a few moments later, he returned. "The surgery is on hold," said the man who brought him back. "The doctor will be in shortly to explain."

As promised the surgeon walked into the room. He was pale and unsettled as he began to speak. "I'm sorry," he said," I couldn't perform your surgery." John and I exchanged glances and looked back at the surgeon. "While I was scrubbing for your surgery I suddenly had a premonition that I should not attempt this. I became unexplainably convinced that I should stop. This has never happened to me before." With that said, the surgeon, visibly shaken, left the room. I sat there in utter amazement until John's words to me broke the eerie silence. "I knew that this was going to happen, I just didn't know how to tell you."

The surgeon's decision was shared with Dr. D who was totally bewildered by the situation. "I spoke with the surgeon," she said, "he is very shaken. He has had some kind of a spiritual message, and nothing I say to him will change his mind. There will be no surgery."

John would have more hospital recovery time before he could be released from the hospital and during that time we were given all the information regarding the transplant. Then one evening during a quiet moment alone together John said, "I have had more than one man can stand in a lifetime-pain, hospitals, surgery, doctors. I am tired and weary of promises for tomorrow. Please, I just want to come home and spend the rest of my life loving my family. Will you support my decision?"

"Home looks so good," John said, as we drove into the driveway. "Thank you honey, I love you."

Events took place at the Riverside Community Hospital intensive care and UCLA medical center, Los Angeles California. July/August 1994.

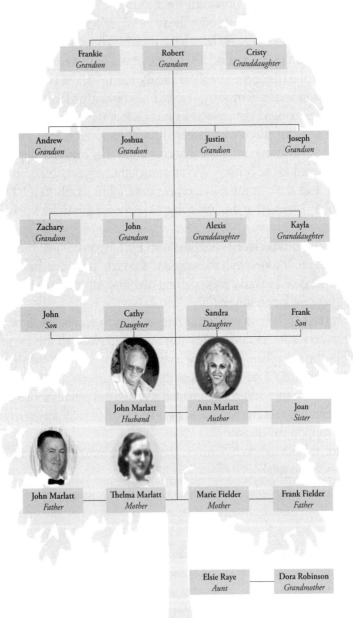

Frankie
Grandson

Robert
Grandson

Cristy
Granddaughter

Andrew
Grandson

Joshua
Grandson

Justin
Grandson

Joseph
Grandson

Zachary
Grandson

John
Grandson

Alexis
Granddaughter

Kayla
Granddaughter

John
Son

Cathy
Daughter

Sandra
Daughter

Frank
Son

John Marlatt
Husband

Ann Marlatt
Author

Joan
Sister

John Marlatt
Father

Thelma Marlatt
Mother

Marie Fielder
Mother

Frank Fielder
Father

Elsie Raye
Aunt

Dora Robinson
Grandmother

Story Eleven

John was essentially a non-believer who felt that life was what we made of it and God was a crutch used by lazy people. Now I watched in amazement as John struggled to deal with some rather unique and unusual abilities that he acquired after the experiences he had in the hospitals. He was frightened and having a difficult time accepting what was happening until this message was shared with him from the other side.

It was John's homecoming and like so many other homecomings, I was looking forward to getting back into some kind of a normal routine. But for the next couple of years, life would be anything but normal or routine.

John didn't speak much about what was happening at first. It caused him more concern and fear than comfort. He had never believed much in anything he couldn't explain, so all these new gifts just confused and frightened him. Soon after his transfer to U.C.L.A., John began to receive visits. At first, the visits were from his mother who died more than 40 years before. Afraid of being labeled crazy he just kept it to himself. The visits and the visitors kept increasing until many dead relatives and some spirits that he could not identify were showing up. It was difficult for him to share this but he finally began to open up and talk about it.

"I know you are going to think I am crazy Ann, but my mother has been here with me so much since this all started happening." He said he was terrified and at first thought that he might be losing his mind. At first I thought it was the illness or the medications. But once he was home for a while it became quite evident that somehow John was experiencing an open door to a spiritual world. I could sense it too. Even the house had a different feeling inside. Every day the feeling grew stronger and I realized that around John, I was experiencing something different and unique. An unseen angelic presence seemed to fill the house and bathe it in love and acceptance. With all the challenges facing our lives there was also a sense of peace in the house.

As the weeks passed, John began to receive more and more spiritual visits and messages. It became a normal daily occurrence for him. I was really enjoying it myself. We had some really interesting discussions during those times. I was overjoyed with the gifts that were given to him and encouraged him to use them to help others. But as this spiritual side grew stronger, he became more withdrawn, calling each new ability a curse.

Several weeks after John's homecoming, John's father took ill. John's dad was devastated that his son had suffered so much in the past and now was going to suffer until he had an early death. He shared with me that he could no longer bear to see John going through all the medical emergencies and the pain that he had to endure. It was his wish to die before his son died. I have always wondered if he had the power to will himself into that coma.

It was difficult for John as we walked into the hospital. He walked to his dad's bedside and reached for his hand. I watched as he let go of his hand as suddenly as he had taken it into his. He touched his dad with one finger then two and then took his hand again. "I can feel everything that is happening to him," John said. "I can feel what he is feeling; I know what he is thinking." We looked at each other in strange amazement. "He feels pain in his hip from lying on that side too long. His eyes are dry and feel gritty; he needs some kind of eye drops. He knows he is dying and wants to go." When he let go of his dad's hand, all the incoming knowledge stopped. John told me he was afraid. "What kind of horrible curse is this that I can feel these things?" He did not like what was happening to him.

The days passed and John was having trouble coping and dealing with his grief surrounding his dad. Each time he got close to tears, he would experience symptoms of his failing heart. He was frightened beyond words, and this gift or whatever it was, continued to grow. Each time John would touch his dad, the gift grew stronger. "Maybe it's just because he is my dad," John said. "I don't seem to feel anything when I touch you or anybody else."

The call came early one morning. John's dad had passed. When we arrived, John walked to his dad's bedside and took his hand in his. "It's gone; he is no longer there." All he felt was emptiness. John's hope was that this was a special, one-time thing between his dad and him. It was a great relief to him when he could no longer feel anything. "I want this curse gone forever," he said.

As the family prepared for the funeral services, John became increasingly afraid.

"I can't handle all of this," he said. "Every time I start to get a little emotional I have pain. Today while at the mortuary, I thought I was having another heart attack. I don't know what to do. I think I should call my family and tell them that I cannot attend the funeral." I convinced him to wait until morning to make any final decision. I offered to get the medicine that the doctor gave us to help keep him calm but he refused to take it. John continued to be anxious and restless; he couldn't sleep. We sat in bed talking for hours. It was 2:00 a.m. when he shared with me his fears of going to sleep.

"I think something is going to happen," he said.

"I think my dad is trying to contact me. He wants to talk to me. I just don't seem to be able to relax and shake this feeling." How it happened at that moment I am unsure to this day, but in the middle of our conversation I fell into a deep sleep.

It was morning when I opened my eyes. I looked over at John; his back was turned to me. He seems quiet enough I thought. As I got out of bed, I realized that John was awake. He was just lying there with a puzzled look on his face. "Oh, you finally decided to wake up," he said teasingly. I was relieved that he seemed to be feeling better. He told me that he had not been asleep and was trying to figure out some information that was given to him in the night.

"What?" I asked, still half asleep. "What are you talking about? What information? From whom?" He turned to me and laughed.

"I have so much to share this morning Ann. Just as you fell asleep, I began to get the strangest feeling about my dad wanting to speak to me again. Suddenly, there he was, only he wasn't alone. He was with my mother. Dad actually did very little talking during the visit," he said amused over the situation. "When they started to talk about you and me and a mission together on this earth, I tried to wake you up to listen."

"Wait!" I said. John's excitement was astounding; it was overtaking my every sense. "And what were you going to tell me? Honey, wake up and put the coffee on. Mom and Dad are here for a visit?" We both started to laugh but then he shared the story that was told to him.

"First of all, they told me not to be afraid to go to the funeral today. They said that I was having some pain but it was not all my heart. Some of it was still from the prior neck surgery and the problems that I have been having with my neck and shoulder. They said it was not my time yet and not to fear. They told me that I would have to live with the pain that I had because that was never going to get any better. They told me that they knew that I was still fearful of losing my legs but that was never going to happen. They told me very sternly to just get use to what I had left.

"They told me I have died six times. I recall once while I was in surgery, I hovered above my body in the corner. I can tell you everything that the doctors were saying. I didn't want to go back into my body. I saw the tunnel and the light and went to it. My mother met me there and brought me back here. I have traveled to the tunnel on other occasions, too, each time

84

meeting my mother who brought me back telling me that it was not yet time for me to come. I can recall all but one and I have been thinking about it all night." I asked if he remembered the time when he was a young boy and in a coma for several days. He was not expected to live through the first night. "That's it," he said, "that is the one time I could not remember. They told me that my job on the earth was not yet finished. Then they began to talk about the two of us. They said your life with Ann was planned long before the two of you ever came to the earth. You both agreed to join and do this mission here. God was very pleased; it has been just the way it was planned. They told me that my dad meeting your dad and going to work for him was not an accident. The meeting was planned to happen just the way it did in order for you and I to meet. They said that the business that your dad started was meant to be the meeting place for the two of us to begin our life and mission together. The mission is not yet completed but when it is finished it will touch the lives of many people on the earth."

"John," I said, "what is this mission that they are speaking about?"

"I am not sure," he said. "They would not give me any details of the future."

"I have always believed it was my choice to stay with you John. Are you telling me that I really had no choice in this?"

"They said that we had paths to choose and we both chose to stay on the path that would successfully complete this mission. We spoke for a very long time. My mom said that she would always stay around me till my time here was complete. She told me that it would not be easy, but that is the way it is. Then they just left, just faded away. I have been lying here thinking about this the rest of the night.

"It's a beautiful day. Come on Ann, it's time to get ready to say our goodbyes to my dad.

John's mother Thelma passed over when John was in his late teens. He shared with me that his mother had come to him on many other occasions when he was very ill, she promised him that she would look over him and be there when it was his time to come home.

Frankie	Robert	Cristy
Grandson	*Grandson*	*Granddaughter*

Andrew	Joshua	Justin	Joseph
Grandson	*Grandson*	*Grandson*	*Grandson*

Zachary	John	Alexis	Kayla
Grandson	*Grandson*	*Granddaughter*	*Granddaughter*

John	Cathy	Sandra	Frank
Son	*Daughter*	*Daughter*	*Son*

John Marlatt	Ann Marlatt	Joan
Husband	*Author*	*Sister*

John Marlatt	Thelma Marlatt	Marie Fielder	Frank Fielder
Father	*Mother*	*Mother*	*Father*

Elsie Raye	Dora Robinson
Aunt	*Grandmother*

Story Twelve

Miracles come in many ways. They are not all handed out by an angel or a guide that mysteriously appears and waves a magic wand. Some miracles are hard work. This miracle is one of those. The gift of health.

I spent a lifetime nurturing and caring for everyone else and put off taking care of myself. I felt that it was some kind of a selfish act to put me first. I was exhausted and felt like I had nothing left to give to me. I turned to food for comfort, something I learned very early in life. It didn't matter if I was happy or sad, I celebrated with food and I commiserated with food. I felt so alone, facing so many challenges. John's health issues were becoming increasingly more serious and difficult for me to face. I realized that I was going to be left alone on this earth to deal with whatever came my way. I was emotionally dying inside, and I was helping myself succeed in physically dying as well.

I found out I had diabetes by surprise like many of us do. I was totally in denial. I hadn't recognized the obvious symptoms. The very thing I was trained to see I had chosen to completely ignore in my own life. I had become very ill with this horrible disease. There were the nights when I felt that if I went to sleep I would surely die. One day the realization of what I was doing to myself made me drop to my knees. I knew I needed to choose: continue the same self-destructive path, or do something about it. The cold hard facts were I didn't want to live like that, and I didn't want to die like that.

My decision to devote myself to my own recovery began a healing in my life. I begged God to show me the path that would lead to my recovery. At first it felt very uncomfortable to put myself on the top of my own needs list. I had to keep reminding myself that I could be of no use to anyone if I became the one that needed to be cared for. I became relentless in my search to find a way back to health, determined to beat this disease. I researched and studied every possible way to get healthy. I made many dietary changes and studied about supplements that would help my body to heal itself. A casual conversation with one of my doctors gave me the final key to my dietary puzzle. He mentioned that diabetes was rare in Korea before the western influence on the country. The increased affluence of the country allowed a diet higher in meats and fat and in turn created a problem with diabetes as big there as it is here. I began to alter recipes to enjoy the foods that I loved and still decrease my fat intake.

My first formal exercise was a Jazzercise class that my daughter Cathy introduced me to. I will never forget what I saw in the mirror the first time

I put on those tights and leotards that she tossed at me. "Wow," I yelled back at her, "I look like one of those characters in the movie Fantasia," and it was not the long necked giraffe that I was referring to. From the first class exercise became a high priority on my list of things to do for me. I really enjoyed those classes and exercise became really addicting. For the first time in more years than I could remember, I was feeling well. As my endurance increased I switched my exercise from the classes to walking. I never realized what an effort it took to walk around the block but I assure you that in the beginning it was not easy.

One day in an effort to give thanks to God for all that he had shown me to do to recover my health, I heard myself making a promise to him. Even as the words fell from my lips I was already trying to find a way to take them back. To this day I have no clue how the words "do a marathon" even became a passing fantasy in my head let alone a promise to God.

The months passed and the town began to call me the walking lady of Glen Avon. At first I was really ridiculed. My husband would tell me that I was an embarrassment to him. Someone would point to me out in the street and ask, "Does anyone know who that crazy lady is?" He would reply, "Nope, never saw her before." Cars would honk and the people in them would point and make some awfully rude remarks. Even the cops began to follow me but they never stopped me. It was rumored that I was much too happy walking out there. I had to be on some kind of substance and maybe I was selling something out of my walking stick. It was really amusing to me so I tried to get them to stop and talk. I would wave and they got to just waving back and then went on their way.

The years passed and what once was ridicule turned into admiration and then to inspiration. You never know what little thing is going to make a difference in life, but I honestly had no idea that I was making any kind of an impact on that neighborhood until I began hearing other kinds of comments. A school bus driver traveling towards me one morning told the children on the bus to look at me walking on the street towards them. She told them that I had turned into an inspiration to the whole crew at the bus barn. It was my determination to keep going no matter the weather that gave them all hope that anything could be accomplished if you just don't give up. One of the children on the bus that day also had something to share with every one on the bus. "That's my Grandma," she proudly announced.

The driver was amazed and now even more inspired to learn that I wasn't as young as they thought I was either. It became the same scenario for the whole area. People began to look for me and look out for me too. Many people still honked their horns but the comments were very different these days. Now instead of stopping on the street to ridicule or harass me, people wanted me to know that I was giving them hope.

And my health issues? After years of using insulin, I no longer needed any medications for the terrible disease that nearly cost me my life. Sometimes miracles don't occur in the way that you would expect. The miracle of my restored health did not happen with a magic wand. It was a lot of hard work and determination, but it was none the less one of the biggest blessings from God that I will ever receive.

It took me many years to realize that it was not a selfish act to take care of my self and put my own needs at the top of my list. Over the years I turned to food for my comfort until it became a huge problem and I was out of control. One day I realized that I didn't want to live that way and I didn't want to die that way. I fought my way back to health but now I realize that the battle for my health would be a life long challenge.

Story One

Explosion on USS Bismarck Sea, Photo February 21, 1945

Story One

Author's Mom and Dad in San Diego at the time of her conception

Story One

Ann's baby picture

Story One

Photo of St. Vibiana Church of author's baptism

Story Four

This is Ann's Grandmother, Dora "Nanny" Robinson

Story Four

Author's Mom and Dad, dancing at Ann's wedding

Story Four

John and Ann (author) at their wedding, April 6, 1963

Story Six

Ann in clown dress in pediatrics

Story Six

Ann as nurse's supervisor in hospital

Story Twenty

John with Granddaughter Kayla

Story Twenty

Kayla at the age of her visits

Story Twenty

Sandra and Kayla - Ann and John's Daughter and Granddaughter

Story Twenty-five

Ann is going to the Marathon starting line, it's still dark outside

Story Twenty-five

And then comes the finish line

Story Twenty-five

The Author and her daughter, Cathy, embracing, after she gave Ann a neckless that said 26.2 miles

Family Photos
Ann (the author) , Joan (sister), Frank III (brother),
Robert "Butch" Fiedler (brother)

Family Photos

Ann and her Grand Children at a Christmas Celebration

Family Photos

John Shopping for Christmas presents

Family Photos

Ann's Grandsons, Joshua (in the back), Joseph,
Zachary and Andrew

Family Photos

Ann's Grand Children

Family Photos

April Cruise, when the Grand Children were a bit older;
Ann, Andrew, Cristy, Kayla, Alexis and Joseph

The Riverside County Record   *Founded in 1955*   909 685-6191

Walking Lady Completes San Diego

✦ Ann Marlatt "The Walking Lady" Spent 10 Ye

By JOHN BALLARD
Record Staff Writer

For the past 10 years, many residents of Jurupa have noticed a lady walking and running on a daily basis up and down Mission Boulevard, Limonite and other streets in the community. To many, Ann Marlatt is affectionately known as "the walking lady," and it is a title well earned. She recently competed in the San Diego Marathon finishing the 26.2 mile event in just over six hours.

But what makes her story so unique is that Marlatt has diabetes and her age, 54, is not typical of a marathon runner.

The Glen Avon woman began a running and weight lifting program a decade ago when she learned she had the life threatening illness. Her weight at the time was almost 300 pounds, and she had to take insulin four times a day to combat the disease.

"I was two months from renal failure," said Marlatt, a clinical coordinator in the wound care center at Methodist Hospital in Arcadia. "I was told by doctors I would have been on dialysis if I didn't do something."

"I didn't want to die that way. I didn't want to live that way," she said, in reference to being down.

vive. "There were days when I would go to bed and think I would

(photo)

ANN MARLATT
...grandmother runs marathon

never get back up."

On the advice of her doctors at her hospital, she began to walk and run for four miles at a time in order to shed the unwanted pounds off her 5'10" frame. As she did this, she brought her weight down to between 150 and 160 pounds. The tremendous loss of weight, combined with a more sensible diet, has

and has ridded the symptoms of the disease from her body.

Also key in her success was a new found faith in God. "I've lived a very spiritual existence the last few years," said Marlatt, a member of Grace Lutheran Church on Mission Boulevard.

It was this faith that would help her through her most trying time - the loss of her husband to heart and lung disease two years ago.

"He was very sick for years," she said. "The healthier I got, the sicker he got." She said his passing was made easier by an earlier visit from Jesus to the both of them, and that helped him to become more accepting of the situation.

"That (visit) just kept me going, and the meaning of it became so clear and is leading me into my future now," she said.

When she began her daily walks around town and began to lose weight, Marlatt said she did not know of the effect that she was having on the people who noticed her.

"Many people have stopped me on the street and have said I have been an inspiration to them," said the grandmother of nine children. "I had no idea I was affecting anybody's life."

And her daily tours down the streets have also found her in some precarious situations. She has had a four run-in with stray dogs, tires

Walking Lady Articles

Ann became an inspiration to the whole town, Glen Avon,
California

102

Family Photos

Ann Marlatt, the author, in the late 1990's

Marathon Runner Article

This is Ann on the runway, after she lost 160 pounds

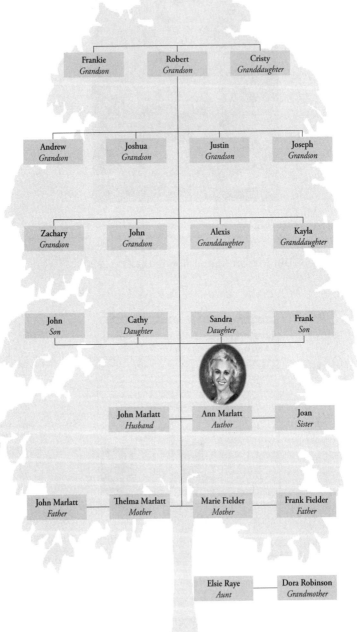

Frankie	Robert	Cristy
Grandson	*Grandson*	*Granddaughter*

Andrew	Joshua	Justin	Joseph
Grandson	*Grandson*	*Grandson*	*Grandson*

Zachary	John	Alexis	Kayla
Grandson	*Grandson*	*Granddaughter*	*Granddaughter*

John	Cathy	Sandra	Frank
Son	*Daughter*	*Daughter*	*Son*

John Marlatt	Ann Marlatt	Joan
Husband	*Author*	*Sister*

John Marlatt	Thelma Marlatt	Marie Fielder	Frank Fielder
Father	*Mother*	*Mother*	*Father*

Elsie Raye	Dora Robinson
Aunt	*Grandmother*

Story Thirteen

Do you retreat into some favorite place when there are so many trials in your life? Most of us have something in our lives that help take us from the daily challenges to a place where we can find renewed strength. My retreat is into music. Was it any wonder that I would understand that messages given to me in this way would help renew my hope and faith?

Denying God's existence was no longer an option for John or me. It was no longer by faith that we knew that God was real. We spoke often now about the reasons for his suffering. John was going through a living hell, a nightmare from which there was no awakening.

It was so difficult for all of us. John's legs burned like hot pokers. He was never again able to wear pants or cover his lower legs with anything - it was just too torturous for him. At times the pain would be more than he could handle. He would sob for relief and beg me to help him. His doctor did not believe in good pain control, fearful that John's heart could not take the stress of the medication. Over the slow moving months there was one crisis after another. Some nights he would be gasping for air, calling out for me to help him as he sat up in his chair. His face was blue and drooping. He was so weak and in so much distress. He was not able to breathe unless he was upright. The air needed to be cold and moving in the room. He had three fans blowing on him. He was in agony.

I had nightmares of running to the cupboard to find some kind of medicine to relieve his symptoms, but the hallway just got longer and longer and I couldn't reach the cupboard. So many times I thought this couldn't last another moment, but it just continued. I sat by him feeling helpless that I couldn't do anything but watch him struggling to survive.

As the months moved slowly by, the symptoms just got worse. He wanted to die so badly that he would pray to God to release him from this. I spent many nights crying my heart out in the driveway as I drove in from work. I was afraid to go in and face the uncertainty of what might be happening. My car became my crying place, the place I could go to renew my strength. I would cry till I couldn't anymore, fix my face, put on my best smile and try to continue to be all that John needed me to be. I would fall asleep out of exhaustion and awake up feeling as tired and overwhelmed as when I went to bed.

"Why God, why? I don't understand. Why didn't you take all his pain and suffering away when you touched him that day? Why did you save his legs and leave him in so much pain? What possible reason could there be for the both of us to be going through all of this?" I realized that I was walking pretty close to the edge. Nothing was making any sense to me anymore. The stress of life was becoming more and more unbearable. Watching John suffer was ripping me apart. Part of me wanted this to be over; I wanted him to die and go home. I wanted to be free of the pain for both of us. Then in the next moment, I would be begging God to heal him and give us another chance at a life together. I was John's comfort on the earth but I was in need of being comforted as well. I longed to be held in his arms. I felt so isolated. I was afraid I couldn't go another step in my life without some kind of reassurance.

It was a cool rainy morning. I was determined to get out and walk anyway. I was out the door before anyone else was awake in the house. I noticed that the rain seemed to stop and the clouds started to part into a beautiful morning. As I moved down the street the black sky was becoming a beautiful blue with big puffy white clouds. It was so wonderful to be out, I just cried. Walking was my time just for me. Sometimes six miles would turn into seven or eight or more. I turned up the music as loudly as I could in the head phones to drown out the world. Music was still my place of refuge. I would listen to the songs of love and I would dream of John being well and dancing with me. That dream became the only thread of hope that I had left. I prayed for signs every day and this day was no different. I knew God was listening and that he heard me. I was so angry with him sometimes.

"Why do you allow this to keep going on?" I would yell. I looked at the now beautiful day and wondered, " Will I ever feel like the clouds of my life will part and bring the sunshine again?" I cried so hard for some kind of answer. Then the song began to play. I hadn't heard it in years.

I can see clearly now the rain has gone.
I can see all obstacles in my way.
Gone are the dark clouds that had me blind.
It's gonna be a bright, bright, sun shining day.
I think I can make it now the pain is gone.
All of the bad feelings have disappeared.
Here is that rainbow I've been praying for.
It's gonna be a bright sun shinning day.

God, could this have been a message from you? Could this be the sign that I have been praying for? I decided that even though it made me stop crying and smile, it was just a coincidence.

I turned the channel on the radio and continued walking when the next song began to play. "*I can see clearly now the rain is gone.*" It stopped me dead in my tracks. I couldn't believe my ears. What are the odds of this, I thought? Still, all the rational arguments against this perfect music being a sign for me flooded my head and I again talked myself out of the message that God had sent to me. It would be just too impossible. I changed the channel on the radio, and now for the third time the song began to play. I listened so intently to the words now.

They just held so much meaning for my life. I didn't know when or how the clouds would lift, but I was reassured that the pain would eventually be just a memory. This storm in our lives would bring the sun. I finally found a measure of peace in all of this pain.

When I arrived back home, I went straight to see John. I told him what had happened that day during my walk. John said that one day we were going to know the reasons but we would have to wait till we cross over to find the answer to that. We were never going to know the reasons why God kept him alive, saved his leg and then allowed such terrible suffering. Accepting the circumstances of our lives with out asking the "why" was the difficult part.

It didn't take me long to realize that I was born with a wonderful voice, a true gift. My grandmother instilled the love of music in my life. By the time I was twelve years old people who heard me sing would ask for an autograph saying that they knew that I would one day be known for my beautiful voice. I met John and married when I was a teenager. I never looked back because somehow I knew that being with him was what I needed to do. But the love of music never left me and it eventually became my place of refuge when life's challenges seem to overwhelm me.

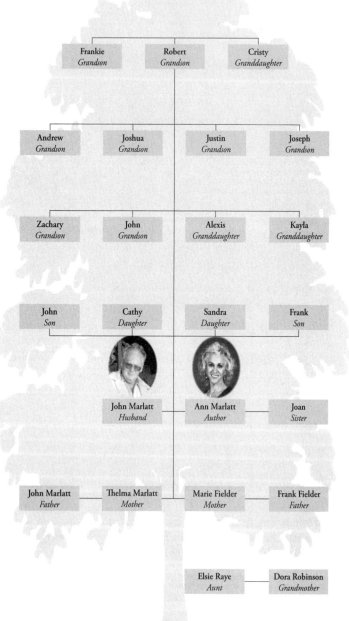

Frankie	Robert	Cristy
Grandson	*Grandson*	*Granddaughter*

Andrew	Joshua	Justin	Joseph
Grandson	*Grandson*	*Grandson*	*Grandson*

Zachary	John	Alexis	Kayla
Grandson	*Grandson*	*Granddaughter*	*Granddaughter*

John	Cathy	Sandra	Frank
Son	*Daughter*	*Daughter*	*Son*

John Marlatt	Ann Marlatt	Joan
Husband	*Author*	*Sister*

John Marlatt	Thelma Marlatt	Marie Fielder	Frank Fielder
Father	*Mother*	*Mother*	*Father*

Elsie Raye	Dora Robinson
Aunt	*Grandmother*

Story Fourteen

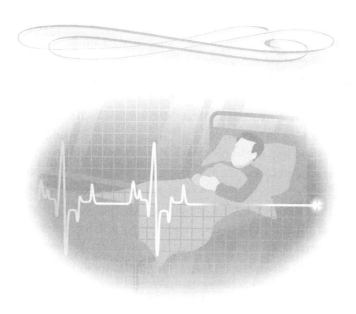

When some one is ill and suffering, the thought to end or help end that person's life can become an issue. The miracles in the hospital left John with his life but it did not end the day-to-day suffering that was wearing us both down. The situation was becoming more unbearable not only for him but also, in all honesty, for me as well.

The months passed and sharing all of these experiences with each other became one of the most joyous things in our lives. John continued to have many spiritual visits from the other side and shared many things with me. The unexplainable gifts that John called his "curses" began to increase again. It first happened one day when a long-time friend gave John a hug to tell him how glad he was to see him up and about. John recoiled and walked away. He told me that Tom had something going on inside his chest. "He will have cancer of the lung and he has a bad heart. I can't even begin to tell you what a terror it is to feel these things," John said. "I thought this was over months ago when my dad died. Now it is coming back."

Over the next few weeks his sensitivity to these things began to grow and grow. He refused to let us finish a pond in the back yard because one of his grandchildren would have had an accident related to it. He came home from the grocery store one day and said that the feeling was getting so strong, that it didn't rely on touch any longer. He felt the sore throat that the clerk was experiencing from across the counter. I encouraged him to cultivate the gift and use it to help others. A friend at work had a son that had been in an auto accident many years before and was "locked" in his body. I asked John to touch him and see if he had a message for his family. John and my co-worker both ultimately refused to allow it, fearful of what they might have learned. John decided to spend most of his time in a self-imposed isolation. He did not want anyone to touch him. He began to talk more and more about dying.

"I just want this to be over," he told me. "I want to die."

I didn't know what to do or say.

"The pain is so bad that it is wearing me down. I can't sleep and I can't seem to find any comfort. Sometimes I feel like I am drowning. I can't breathe and the air I do take in doesn't do any good. I never know how bad the pain is going to get and it scares me to think about having to go through that. I can't handle this anymore."

He was hanging on by a thread. I couldn't believe what he had been living through over the past year. Between the pain and suffering from breathing, he could barely manage to get around anymore. I prayed for answers for him. I prayed for answers for the both of us.

"God, I don't know what to do. I don't know how to help him anymore. He's asking to die and I don't know how to help him."

I walked and walked that morning. As usual the music in my headphones was so loud that I couldn't even hear a horn honking. Suddenly I heard a rustling noise in the bushes. I ignored it, thinking it was in my tape. Hearing the noise again made me go back and look through the bushes. There it was a little bird, pure white, either a baby pigeon or a dove. It seemed to be struggling as I gently removed him from the bushes. He was injured. He must have been hit by a car and knocked into the bushes. I tried to handle him as gently as possible. I wanted to help him but I felt powerless. The injuries were so severe that I could not comfort him. He was lying in my hands and kept lifting his head to look me straight in the eyes. I was crying for him.

He was in pain and made little noises each time I moved with him. I tried to cover his eyes so he wouldn't be frightened. I knew he couldn't understand what was happening and there was nothing I could do to tell him. "God, what do I do," I cried. I walked with him in my hands for the longest time. I began to realize that there was something more than an injured bird in my hand. I could feel God all around me. I begged God to give me the strength to put an end to his suffering. I knew that God would not want any creature to suffer. I wanted to snap his neck to put him out of his misery.

"Okay, little bird, here it goes…I can't do it!" I cried out. "I just can't do it. I'm sorry little bird; I just can't take your life. I can only hold you and try to comfort you until you die." Suddenly I knew. Awareness came over me as those words fell from my mouth. "God, I understand what you are showing me." I was shaking as I realized that I nearly put the little bird to death but stopped short because I just couldn't do it. I had this feeling of sheer terror as I thought, God, what if I would have done it? The sense of terror was replaced by a feeling of peace with the message, "But you didn't do it, did you?" I realized that there was nothing I could do except just be with them, the little white bird and with John. It was my answer. I looked now at the little life struggling in my hands. I began to pray. Please, God, don't let this little bird or John suffer on this earth one breath longer than they need to. I looked into the little bird's eyes as he stared into mine. With that he lifted his head, took one last breath, slowly fell back in my hand and died.

I carried him for the longest time. I didn't know where to put him. It just didn't seem right to drop him in a trashcan or put him in the fields. I came upon a rock wall that was surrounding a self-storage building. I placed him at the cornerstone of the building facing the big rock. I gave him to God.

I couldn't wait to talk to John and ran the rest of the way home. John and I spoke about the little bird and all the meaning around it. I knew that the one thing that I could not do was to help John take his own life. I told him that I would stick by him and support any decision that he made except suicide. God made it perfectly clear that the decision to kill himself, or to have anyone assist him in a suicide, was not an option.

We no longer had the need to know why all this was happening, we just needed to hang onto the fact that God was never going to leave us!

The little bird was found on Mission Blvd. and Pedley Street in Glen Avon, California, just across the street from Angels of Grace Church. To this day I don't know how I could possibly have heard that little bird rustling in the bushes. It was so young I couldn't tell if it was a dove or a pigeon but the lesson that it taught me that day will stay with me for the rest of my life.

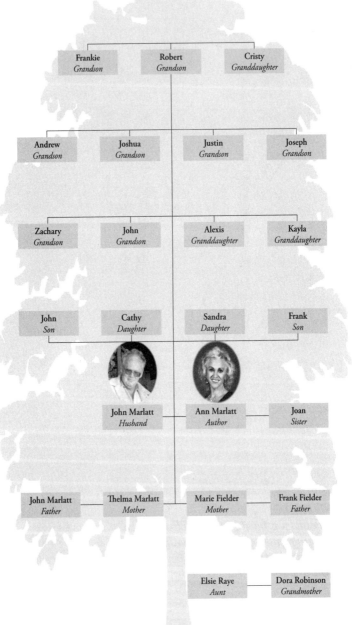

| Frankie | Robert | Cristy |
| *Grandson* | *Grandson* | *Granddaughter* |

| Andrew | Joshua | Justin | Joseph |
| *Grandson* | *Grandson* | *Grandson* | *Grandson* |

| Zachary | John | Alexis | Kayla |
| *Grandson* | *Grandson* | *Granddaughter* | *Granddaughter* |

| John | Cathy | Sandra | Frank |
| *Son* | *Daughter* | *Daughter* | *Son* |

| John Marlatt | Ann Marlatt | Joan |
| *Husband* | *Author* | *Sister* |

| John Marlatt | Thelma Marlatt | Marie Fielder | Frank Fielder |
| *Father* | *Mother* | *Mother* | *Father* |

| Elsie Raye | Dora Robinson |
| *Aunt* | *Grandmother* |

Story Fifteen

John struggled between his desire to live and the suffering that created his wish to die. His communication with the "other side" had increased to the point that he seemed to be living between two worlds. His decision to take matters into his own hands and create a shortcut to end his suffering ended with this Divine intervention.

"I want to die." Those words cut through my heart like a knife. My own mixed emotions tore me apart. I was crushed by the weight of what was happening in our lives. Part of me longed for this nightmare to be over, and I felt a deep sense of guilt for my thoughts. John's suffering was endless. It never gave us a moment's peace. I thought about ways to help the both of us to cope with the never-ending stress that filled our lives.

Maybe a trip to our favorite campsite might help the both of us, I suggested. It was a very beautiful place where we both felt a sense of peace by just being there. I thought about all the wondrous trips we made to that lake, how he loved to sit at the water's edge with that fishing pole. Our grandchildren would be all around him, happy and laughing. I could picture those beautiful memories and thought that it may make a little difference if we went back there now. It was my plan to help John over this difficult time but it soon became apparent that he had quite a different agenda in mind.

"I promised God that I would not take my own life, but I don't think it is wrong to stop taking my medications. If I am meant to live, I will live with out the medications. If not, I will finally be free from this suffering and die." I was struggling with his decision. I just hadn't a clue what to do. I remember praying. I promised John I would always be by his side and support his decisions but I didn't know if I could live with the consequence of this action. We arrived at the campsite and set up for our stay. Somehow things just seemed to be a little easier to deal with when we were standing in such a beautiful place, watching the sunset over the lake. It was breath-taking there.

From the moment we arrived, John seemed to have an increase in visits from the other side. We were standing at the doorway of our motor home, just going outside, when John suddenly stopped and turned to me.

"You need to go back to church and stay there," he said.

I nearly choked over the words that just came from his mouth. "John, I can't believe I just heard what you said. You have battled with me for more than thirty years now about finding a church home. You have had nothing but bad things to say about any church that I have ever tried to attend. Now you suddenly turn to me and tell me to go back to church?"

John smiled and said, "Well, it isn't a message from me, it's from them."

"Oh, I see, it's from them. And whom, may I ask, are they?"

He was laughing now. "I don't know. They didn't give me names." He was getting terribly amused by all the little messages and visits he was getting these days. I have to admit, I just loved to stand in the fallout of the blessings that he was receiving.

"Just where am I supposed to go?"

"Well, they didn't give me directions."

I just looked at him and busted up laughing. I swear if anyone ever heard us having these conversations they would surely believe that we were both crazy.

It was the middle of the week when I pulled out the phone book to try to find a new church home. I had gone to church in our neighborhood for a couple of years awhile back, but I left there less than pleased with the way my daughter and I were treated by the members. I swore I would never step foot in that place again. I thought about the church. I passed it each morning that I walked. The little bird I found dying was found just across the street from that church. Nope, that was not an option. I wrote down the names of several churches in the Riverside area and decided I would set off early on Sunday morning to find a new church home.

It was Saturday evening. Throughout the day I had been experiencing an uncomfortable uneasiness in the motor home. I could not shake the feeling that something was going to happen. Maybe it was just John's increased symptoms since he had stopped taking his medications. He was suffering more now. He was not able to move around very well. He was totally unable to lie down in the bed. He spent much of his time sitting in front of the TV, propped up on the sofa with many pillows. My own emotions were twisted and turned into knots. I found it painful to watch him like this.

By Saturday night the inside of the motor home had become a very eerie place. I went to bed early, leaving John sitting on the sofa watching TV. Something strange was happening. I didn't know what it could be, but it was enormous and made me feel reduced to a child.

I fell asleep but awakened in the middle of the night. The feeling was even stronger now. I was frightened by what I was sensing in the motor home, and I couldn't figure out what it was. I got up and walked to the front of the motor home where John was sitting. The TV was out, which was very unusual because he never turned it off. He was not wearing his glasses and his eyes were open, fixed and staring into space. Something was happening in there, I just didn't know what. I suddenly just wanted to run. My feet barely touched the floor as I flew back into the bedroom, jumped into the bed and pulled the covers up over my head in an effort to not see or hear or feel what was happening. Strangely, I fell instantly back to sleep. When I awakened in the morning I went to talk to John. John asked me why I removed his glasses and turned off the TV. I told him I hadn't and I told him the way I had found him sitting and staring in the night. I told him something pretty awesome was happening in there during the night. I don't think that he really believed me.

John was really suffering that morning. He could barely sit up. I offered to stay but he insisted that I leave and carry out what I was told to do about finding a church. I left with the feeling that this was not going to be an ordinary day. I drove all over Riverside and checked all five of the churches on my list. The first church started an hour before; I would have to keep searching. The second turned out to be a Korean speaking church. The third one on the list I could never find, and I just didn't feel like I belonged at the fourth and fifth. I was just driving around when I realized that I was in my neighborhood and heading for the church I swore I would never go into again. I remember the strange sensation that I had when I pulled into the driveway. I put aside my angry feelings about the people there and went inside. The service was just about to begin. The pastor was not the same man that was there before; I was rather grateful for that. Not many of the same people were still there. The church seemed strangely empty. I sat through the service and wondered the whole time what I was doing there. I guess I was just expecting some big miracle to happen in front of my eyes.

I began to cry as I headed for my car but decided to go back and speak to the pastor. I told him that I knew he would think me crazy. I then shared the whole story about John, our visit from Jesus, and all the strange things that were happening in our lives. He was so kind to me. I asked him if he thought I was nuts. He smiled and said not at all. "In fact," he said, "I am fascinated with what you have been through. God is using you for a purpose. Now tell me, what can I do for you today?"

I looked at him in total frustration. "Do for me? You are supposed to tell me what I am doing here today. God sent me here, now you ask me why?" We both laughed at what was obviously a question that would not be answered so quickly. He wished me well and I promised to return.

Driving back to the motor home was difficult. I didn't know how to face John. He was so ill now, I didn't know what to expect. I had no answer as to why I was told to go to church and stay there. I was afraid to face what I might find back at the motor home as well. The feelings of the overwhelming enormous power that was present yesterday began to fill my thoughts. What could it have been? I parked the car and went inside. John was sitting there waiting for me.

"Ann, I have good news and bad news."

"Okay," I said. "I will bite. What is the good news?"

"The good news is I started to take my medicine again. I am feeling a little better now than I did when you left." I was very pleased but rather surprised.

"What is the bad news?" I asked.

"I have started to take my medicine again," he said.

"I don't understand, John. What do you mean?"

"Ann, I wanted to die so much and I know how hard this has been on you, too. I know you want me to die, too. I know you need to get on with some kind of life. That is why this is the good news and the bad news." I began to cry. I realized that what he had to say was true.

"You were right about what was happening in the night. The minute you walked out of the door this morning something began to happen in here. I began to feel something strange. There was a powerful and unexplainable presence that seemed to fill the motor home. After a time I found myself frozen in the chair. I was staring off into another place when suddenly a huge and powerful male voice surrounded me. He was very stern as he spoke to me.

'John,' he said, 'you have two choices. You can continue to take the medicine and although you will not get any better, you will still be able to get around as you have been doing. Or, you can choose to not take the medicine and you will feel the effects of the illness to the point where you will not even be able to get out of bed. The choice is yours, but either way you will live with the consequences of your choice. It is not yet your time to come home.' Then whatever it was began to fade and I was released from the chair.

"I have never in my life felt anything as powerful as what was here with me. It was the most commanding thing I have ever experienced. You must have awakened in the night and interrupted what was happening. It came to me so quickly after you left. I am surely overwhelmed by God's awesome power. It didn't take me very long to decide to take my medicine again. Now tell me, where were you led? What church does he want you to attend?"

The campground is at Bonelli Park also known as Puddingstone lake in San Dimas, California. It was and is one of the most beautiful places that I have ever stayed. The feel of the place is like being in the wilderness or a mountain resort yet it is nestled in the heart of the city. I have met up with all types of wild life in the area including raccoons, skunks, coyotes, and even a mountain lion or two.

The church is Angels of Grace Church. 8877 Mission blvd. Glen Avon California, Pastor Ken Puccio. A small plaque still hangs in the entry bearing Johns name along with other members who have passed on.

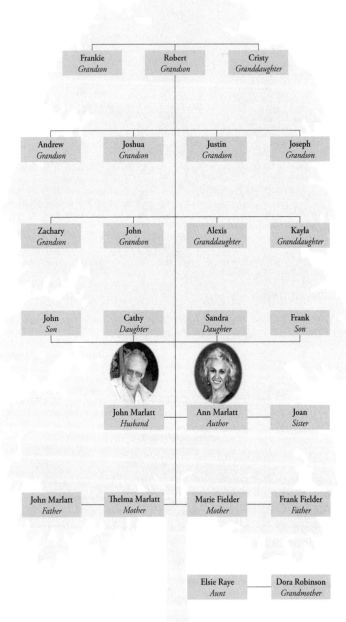

| Frankie
Grandson | Robert
Grandson | Cristy
Granddaughter |

| Andrew
Grandson | Joshua
Grandson | Justin
Grandson | Joseph
Grandson |

| Zachary
Grandson | John
Grandson | Alexis
Granddaughter | Kayla
Granddaughter |

| John
Son | Cathy
Daughter | Sandra
Daughter | Frank
Son |

| John Marlatt
Husband | Ann Marlatt
Author | Joan
Sister |

| John Marlatt
Father | Thelma Marlatt
Mother | Marie Fielder
Mother | Frank Fielder
Father |

| Elsie Raye
Aunt | Dora Robinson
Grandmother |

Story Sixteen

Accepting that our life together was coming to an end was the most difficult thing that I ever had to face. Now life as I knew it would end and I would be destined to walk a new path.

In our final time together on this earth, finding a church home helped me to experience a deeper sense of peace and comfort than I had ever known. Still, I wanted answers from God and raised questions to him constantly. I wanted some rational explanation of everything that John and I had been going through. I wanted to know from the depths of my being why I was sent to that church.

John was actively seeking the "why's" in his life, but remained very resistant to going to church. He still had many negative feelings regarding religion and the need to go to any church. One Sunday morning, out of his pain and need for answers he cried out to me to wait for him, stating that maybe he would find some kind of answer there. He made his way to his feet and began to change his clothes. I silently watched him struggle, standing by in case he needed me. I ran outside and loaded his motorized cart in the car.

I wanted this to be a positive experience for him. I had never realized how I longed for my husband to join me in church until that day. It would be one of the biggest blessings I ever received. He sat there and listened and then a wonderful thing happened- he wanted to come back again. John and I began to attend church every week. One Sunday, to my surprise, he got up and addressed the other members. He told of how he had fought acknowledging the reality of God his whole life until he had the blessing of the visit from Jesus.

"I thought you people were all just weak and crazy. I thought you were all just looking for some kind of crutch, an excuse for a lack of responsibility for your own lives. I was so wrong," he said. "I have wasted so many years of my life with the wrong ideas about God. God is real and I have only just found him." John officially became a member of the church that day. I saw such peace come over him. John loved going to church now. Our children and grandchildren were joining us. It was John's greatest pleasure to listen to them sing and act out the little bible songs.

Things began to change at home, too. I could sense his acceptance of his situation. I could see him actively preparing for his life to come to an end. It was me who couldn't face what was really going to be the inevitable end. I thought about all the dreams and promises for the future that I had more than thirty years before. There was so much in my life that was undone. I hurt more inside than I could ever begin to describe. John began to push me out of his life. He told me he wanted me to grieve for him now before he died so it wouldn't be so difficult for me after. I felt cheated. "Don't rob me of our last times together, please, John," I begged. He wouldn't or couldn't hear what was in my heart when I tried to speak to him, so I wrote it in a letter and hung it on the bathroom mirror for him to find.

Please, I wrote, *grant me these few last requests before you leave me on this earth alone.* He read the letter and asked to be alone for the night to think about what he needed to do. The following day John stood quietly in front of me with his response.

"Ann, I know what is in your heart and that is going to make my answers seem unkind and painful, but I think it would be so much crueler to you to respond in any other way. There are things in life that are not meant for us to share. You wrote that your greatest wish is for me to be healed so we can finally begin to have something in our lives besides pain, suffering and difficult challenges. Even though I realize that this was not a question but rather a wish from your heart, we both know that it is not really something that we have the power to change. I think you know that it's a prayer that just won't be answered in the way you want it to be answered. We both know what is going to happen here and we need to accept it.

"You are seeking answers to questions in our relationship that have been in your heart for many years. Other than the issues we have already spoken about, the time for answers are gone. I can't answer any more simply because I have no more answers to give you. I have no more capacity to help you here.

"You ask me to hold you. You need to feel my comforting arms around you, to allow you to cry to help you to get through all of this. I cannot do that Ann. I will never hold you again. I just cannot.

"Lastly Ann, I hear and I understand your request for me to fulfill your one lifelong desire: you ask me for just one dance. I know that you have waited for this dance since our wedding day more than thirty-three years ago. Oh Ann, I will never give you that one dance. You have to know that there is no more hope of the relationship that you need between the two of us. But I know that there is another man out there who will be the husband to you that I was never able to be. It will be up to you to allow yourself to find him when I am gone. I pray that God will not allow you to be alone here too long. And Ann, I will be watching and smiling when you have your first dance together."

It was the worst of times for me. My every waking moment seemed like a never-ending hell. I was so afraid that I would go over the edge of sanity and never come back. My dreams, wishes and prayers were the only hope I had left and now even they were gone. My emotions overwhelmed me. I was so frustrated and hurt. I didn't understand any of this. I needed to feel God in my life more than I ever needed him before, but I couldn't seem to find him. I felt the weight of the earth crushing the life from me and felt that the weight of a single feather added to me would surely break me into pieces. I felt my frustration turning into anger and then turning inward to a deep depression. The depression held me hostage, bound tightly in a cocoon and suspended me in emotional and spiritual pain. But the cocoon that was wrapped so tightly around me, allowed me time. Then time allowed me to realize that just like with the little bird dying in my hand, nothing else could be done, and that led me to the path of acceptance. I had taken the first steps in walking down my new path.

Our last days together were both blessed and difficult. I took him to the hospital that Sunday evening after spending the kind of day that we both had come to cherish. We shared communion together at church and watched as our grandchildren, using their invisible fishing poles into the waters of the life, sang John's favorite hymn, "Fishers of Men." He laughed until the tears of gratitude ran gently down his cheek. John would spend the next few days in intensive care, and I spent them in denial. Even though the doctor told me that John would never come home again, I chose not to believe it. "I've heard those words before," I told him. "John will recover again, you'll see. Yes, he will recover." I was certain of this.

I was working that night and visited his room whenever I could get away. Towards the end of my shift I went in and said goodnight. An hour later I gathered my belongings and headed for the car. A little voice began to nag me to return to say one last good night. I came back inside the hospital and started towards his room. As I entered his room I heard that same voice in my head say, "If you never saw him on this earth again, what would you like him to know?" The message startled me but I wouldn't allow myself to believe that he was really going to die.

I held his hand and told him, "I love you, and I am glad I chose to spend my life with you." He asked me to stay but I chose to leave. Shortly after I arrived home, the phone call came.

It was two years, two months and two weeks after our visit with Jesus that John went home to be with God. I miss you John. Perhaps one day, I will dance.

John Wilbert Marlatt my husband of more than thirty three years passed away on September 19, 1996 at Greater El Monte Hospital, So El Monte California. .

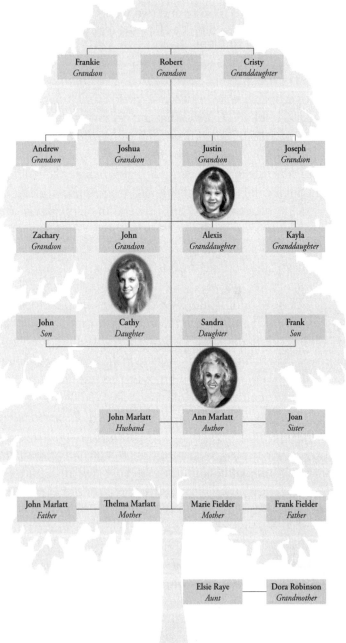

Frankie	Robert	Cristy
Grandson	*Grandson*	*Granddaughter*

Andrew	Joshua	Justin	Joseph
Grandson	*Grandson*	*Grandson*	*Grandson*

Zachary	John	Alexis	Kayla
Grandson	*Grandson*	*Granddaughter*	*Granddaughter*

John	Cathy	Sandra	Frank
Son	*Daughter*	*Daughter*	*Son*

John Marlatt	Ann Marlatt	Joan
Husband	*Author*	*Sister*

John Marlatt	Thelma Marlatt	Marie Fielder	Frank Fielder
Father	*Mother*	*Mother*	*Father*

Elsie Raye	Dora Robinson
Aunt	*Grandmother*

Story Seventeen

My nature was to help others, but those days I felt like I had nothing left to give to anybody. I felt that my life had become purely survival. I wondered if I would ever feel like I could help another person again.

After John's death so many things changed for me. That magical angelic feeling that was present in the house just seemed to disappear and I was hit with the realization that I was living on earth and not in some heavenly place. It was weighing so heavily on my mind as I began my morning walk. I'm surprised I could find the strength to walk, I felt so emotionally cocooned and restrained. I thought I had no capacity left to give anything to anybody. It was all turned inward in an effort to just survive. My greatest rewards centered on helping others and I wanted to find my way back to feeling whole again. I prayed for healing so I could begin to feel like I was alive.

I noticed the man walking on the other side of the street. He was middle aged, a bit pudgy and out of shape. He was moving very slowly in the same direction as me but seemed very tired and unstable. I saw him from a distance but I caught up to him quickly. As I watched him, he turned to J-walk across the street toward me. It was the main street in town and the traffic moved very quickly. I watched him to be sure that he could make it across. There wasn't a car in sight as I looked up and down the street. I remember thinking that it was a good thing that the street was never really very busy. The man seemed a little out of place. His clothes - an old suit and vest - just didn't seem to fit the times. He had what I thought was a brief case but as he approached it looked more like an old tawny colored saddlebag. He reached me and tried to step up on the curb but was just too tired and short of breath. So instead, he turned and sat down on the curb. I watched as he opened the saddlebag and then closed it again. It all happened so fast.

"Are you all right?" I asked.

"Yes," he said, "I am fine."

"You don't look fine. Are you sure you don't need help?"

"No, I am fine. I just need to sit for a moment."

"Are you having any pain? Is there anything I can do to help you?"

"No, I am fine."

"Well, if you are sure."

I turned to walk away but I was so uncomfortable leaving him sitting on the curb in trouble. What was I thinking? I took only a few steps down the sidewalk before I knew what I had to do. I wasn't going to take no for an answer. I turned to face him but he was nowhere to be seen. I looked up and down the street. There was no place that he could have gone without me seeing him. The sidewalk was in front of a self-storage building with a tall brick wall around it. The field on both side of the storage area was empty. I looked across the street. Even if he was a marathon runner he couldn't have crossed the street as fast as I had turned to come back. Besides, I could see up and down the street. The only houses had chain-link fencing across the front yards. I would have been able to see him. There had been no cars going by that could have picked him up. I began to have the most eerie feeling. I stood there wondering what had just happened. Could this have been some kind of an angel? A little voice in my head was asking me about what had happened to the woman who had lost the capacity to help someone in distress. I remember thinking how wonderful it would have been to share this with John. I decided to call the kids later.

"Hi, Mom," Cathy said as I picked up the phone. "Talk about unsettling moments. The strangest thing happened this afternoon."

"It must be the day for it," I said. "Something really strange happened to me this morning." She continued.

"I drove over to the bus stop to pick up Alexis. I pulled the car off the road and looked all around to make sure Alexis wasn't waiting there for me. I just turned my head and was suddenly startled by a knock on my window. Standing there was this very strange man. I have no idea where he came from. He was nowhere to be seen a moment before. He was wearing some kind of a plaid shirt that looked like it was straight out of the last century. He looked very tired. I was somewhat overwhelmed by his presence and had this feeling that I should help him. I began to roll down my window just as the school bus arrived and let Alexis off. I asked if he needed help. He smiled at me and said, 'Everything is going to be ok.' I turned from the window for a split second as Alexis reached the door. When I looked back up, he was gone. I looked all over for him. He was just gone. I don't have a clue in the world who this man was. I can't seem to get his message out of my mind. Was he telling me that he was ok or was he giving me a message that I would be ok?"

"Tell me, Cathy, did you notice if he was carrying anything?"

"Wow, Mom, funny you should ask. I know this sounds a little nuts but I would swear that he was carrying something that resembled an old leather saddlebag. So Mom, tell me - what happened to you today?"

This funny little man was first seen by me close to my home and then by my daughter close to hers.

133

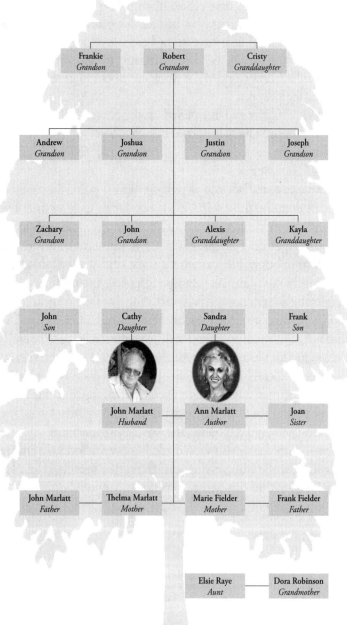

Frankie	Robert	Cristy
Grandson	Grandson	Granddaughter

Andrew	Joshua	Justin	Joseph
Grandson	Grandson	Grandson	Grandson

Zachary	John	Alexis	Kayla
Grandson	Grandson	Granddaughter	Granddaughter

John	Cathy	Sandra	Frank
Son	Daughter	Daughter	Son

John Marlatt	Ann Marlatt	Joan
Husband	Author	Sister

John Marlatt	Thelma Marlatt	Marie Fielder	Frank Fielder
Father	Mother	Mother	Father

Elsie Raye	Dora Robinson
Aunt	Grandmother

Story Eighteen

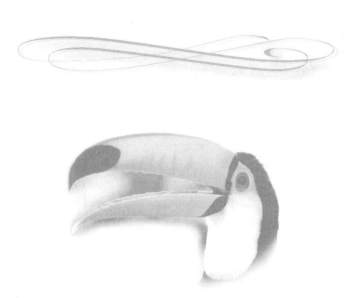

John loved birds and raised many different kinds. I loved toucan birds so John planned to add a toucan to the aviary. John died before he was able to give me that gift. The birds were all gone now and the empty flight cages in the yard became a constant reminder that our life together was gone, too. We shared such a spiritual connection the last couple of years of his life. Now I struggled with the realization that he would be gone from me forever.

In the middle of the night, my eyes popped open. The dream was so real. I lay there thinking about John. It had been over a year since he died. I had been so sure that John would find a way to communicate with me after he died but it never happened. We shared such a spiritual connection, especially during the last couple years of his life, that I was surprised that it all ended. Twice I awakened to what I thought was his voice yelling out my name, but nothing followed.

I was having the usual nighttime dream. I rarely remember anything I dream but this was different somehow. In the middle of the dream John just came walking in. I don't even remember what I was dreaming; it just wasn't anything significant or important, nor did it have anything to do with John before he walked into the dream. He was carrying four large birds: a white cockatoo, a pink cockatoo, a blue and gold Macaw and a Toucan. He walked toward me and stood in front of me. He told me that he brought me a present. He held out his left arm to me and said, "Here Ann, this is the toucan that you wanted."

When we were planning the landscape of our backyard we had planned to put in a large bird flight area. John raised many exotic birds and I wanted to have a toucan to add to the collection. He then turned and walked away, out of my sight, and my dream continued. The vision was so vivid. The colors were so clear and crisp. It was like going from black and white to crystal clear color and back again. It awakened me and I wondered for the longest time if it was real or just a dream.

A week later at work, an old friend's name suddenly popped into my head. I hadn't spoken to her in months. Feeling suddenly compelled to call her I went to my office and dialed her number. She said she wasn't surprised to hear from me. She had been thinking about me all week and decided she should call me. She said she had a visit from John in the form of a dream. I became quite interested and asked her when it had happened. It happened to be the same night that John gave me the toucan in my dream. She told me that John said he came to give her a present. He handed her a white cockatoo.

My curiosity got the better of me and I asked her, "How many birds did John have with him when he gave you the cockatoo?"

"Only one," she said, "the bird that he gave to me." I told her that John had brought me a toucan the same night, but when I saw him he had four birds with him. We both laughed as we spoke about John. Who got the other two birds remains a mystery to this day.

Over the years birds have become a very big part of my life. When I am feeling down and missing John, I will often see a dove or a pair of doves around me during the day to remind me that just because we cannot see a loved one that has passed over, they are still with us.

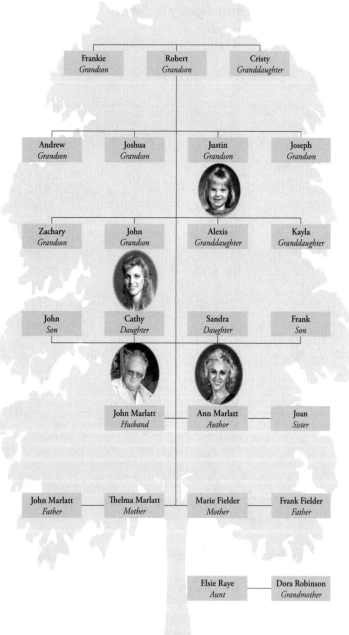

Frankie
Grandson

Robert
Grandson

Cristy
Granddaughter

Andrew
Grandson

Joshua
Grandson

Justin
Grandson

Joseph
Grandson

Zachary
Grandson

John
Grandson

Alexis
Granddaughter

Kayla
Granddaughter

John
Son

Cathy
Daughter

Sandra
Daughter

Frank
Son

John Marlatt
Husband

Ann Marlatt
Author

Joan
Sister

John Marlatt
Father

Thelma Marlatt
Mother

Marie Fielder
Mother

Frank Fielder
Father

Elsie Raye
Aunt

Dora Robinson
Grandmother

Story Nineteen

Young children have a natural ability to stay connected with life on the other side. How many of us try to persuade them that their imaginary friends are not real, or stop them when they casually mention that they saw a loved one that has passed? Some of our greatest lessons can come out of the mouths of babes.

"Grandma! Grandma!" six-year-old Alexis shouted as she excitedly ran through the front door. "I have to tell you about my dream." She paused, and with a puzzled look on her face said, "Only my dream wasn't a dream. "I was in bed asleep and woke up in the night. My dog Taz was sleeping by my bed. I was thinking about Grandpa and crying and suddenly there he was standing by my bed. I was so glad to see him again. Taz saw Grandpa, too. He got scared and yelped and whimpered and then he ran to the corner. Grandpa and I laughed about it. We talked and I told him what was happening. I told him that you cry for him all the time. He said he knew that you were crying. I told him that I was sad because nothing was the same anymore. Christmas was always the happiest and best day for me when he was here, now it's different."

"He asked me if I wanted to go with him to his home for a visit to play. I was so excited, I said yes. He said that we would stop to see you first, Grandma. He held my hand and we started to leave and that was the only time I got scared. I looked down and saw myself asleep and didn't know how that could happen. Grandma, we came to see you," she said giggling. "I sat by the door and watched while Grandpa went over and lay down next to you. You were asleep on Grandpa's side of the bed. He put his arm around you and talked to you but you just stayed asleep. He told me it was time to go and he took my hand. I began to feel like I was flying. It was a tickling feeling. I giggled. I saw clouds and beautiful pink and purple sky. The sky was different; it wasn't the same color blue up there like here. Then we came to a big gate or a big door. There was a path to it and it was all white. It was really bright and it was shining. The light was as bright as the sun and it was shining thru the gate. The first place that Grandpa took me was to your house, Grandma.

"It was so big. It was two stories high. It had lots of rooms. We didn't go inside. We just looked around at the house. I laughed and told Grandpa that it had no roof. How could Grandma live there? Grandpa said it wasn't finished yet. But it would be done when you lived there. There were miles of rose gardens around your house. Just like you like, Grandma. They were so beautiful. They smelled so pretty. There was a pond in your backyard like the one that Grandpa was building for you at your house, but this one was finished, and it had lots of fish in it. I saw lots of crosses up there. There are crosses everywhere.

"Grandma, if someone wants to see you they just picture you in their mind and they are with you or see you. They come here to be with us during fun times, too. Like when we go to Disneyland or to the park or something. They know what is happening. They know when you are talking about them. When you pray and say a person in your prayer, it goes to God and to the person.

"Then Grandpa took me fishing. I think because that is what we liked to do best before. The fishing place was like some kind of a compartment. Everything there is in compartments. It was like a pond but different. It's hard to tell you about it. The water was not like our color blue; it was just pure. Nothing up there is dirty. We sat on a ledge at the edge of the pond but our feet never touched the water. Even the water didn't look like water. It was so pure and there was no dirty part. I can't describe what it is like there.

"We laughed and played and then Grandpa took me to see the angels. There were great big angels and little tiny ones that you could barely see. All the angels took good care of the baby ones. I saw this tiny new angel in this great big bed. Some angels had wings and some angels didn't. I saw a big room that was filled with wings. The wings were so delicate. You can't touch them. They are held on this special wall by these funny nails. The nails have holes that air goes through, and that's how they stayed on the wall. They were not all white. They were different colors, and gold and silver.

"Then the angels were so nice to me. They took me to a special place. There were no hills to climb but we climbed up clouds. There were big houses all around in a circle facing the middle. We walked into a big building and they took me into this big room. It was so beautiful in there. It was filled with papers and books. The angels put me in a big chair. They put a book in my hands. I looked at the words and I was kind of scared because I didn't know how to read them. I told them that the words were too big for me to read. The angels put a bracelet on my hand. And when I looked at the book again, I could read it real good. I read and read the book. I am not sure what it was all about, but I think it was about my life. When they took the bracelet off, I could not remember too much. The angels took me to another place. They sang to me. It made me feel good.

"I saw Jesus' mother, her name was Mary. She was real nice to me. I told her about my brother and sister. I told her my brother had messy hair. She laughed and said Jesus' hair would get messy, too, when he was a boy. She said it would stick straight up. I saw Jesus; he was carrying a baby lamb in his arms. He was so big there. Everything was so happy. No one was sad. I remember looking down sometimes through the clouds and seeing myself asleep in my house. I didn't know how I could do this. Then Grandpa said it was time to go home. He took me by the hand and began to take me home. I could feel myself flying again. Then I was alone but I wasn't afraid. When I woke up, I was back at home. I was so excited, I ran to tell my mommy about my dream that wasn't a dream. Grandma, you don't need to cry anymore. I know that Grandpa comes to see you all the time. You get to see Grandpa in your special dreams that aren't really dreams. You don't need to miss him anymore."

Over the next few months, Alexis would have many special visits with her Grandpa. Then came the last visit that she would experience.

"I woke up in the night and I went out to the kitchen to get a glass of milk. I was awake and walking back to my room. The next thing I knew I was gone to Grandpa's house again. I don't remember going to sleep and I don't remember going there, I was just there. This time Grandpa took me to see the angels again. The angels were so nice. They held my hand and took me to a special place. They carried me over the water to a big rock and left me there. I looked around and there was water all over. I was not afraid but I was alone on the rock."

"I saw Jesus standing there. Then the angels started to sing. They sang and sang like at a celebration, and then the angels came and baptized me. I was so happy to be there. There were thousands of angels around me singing. The music was not like anything from here, it was more beautiful then I can tell you. Then Grandpa brought me home again. When I woke up, I was asleep in the living room and my milk glass was empty. I don't even remember drinking the milk," she giggled.

Alexis is now a beautiful teenage girl and the door closed forever on dreams that weren't dreams.

Over the years that followed I tried endlessly to help Alexis retain the memory of her special visits with her grandpa; but as time passed the memories began to fade until she could no longer recall the wonderful dreams that weren't dreams.

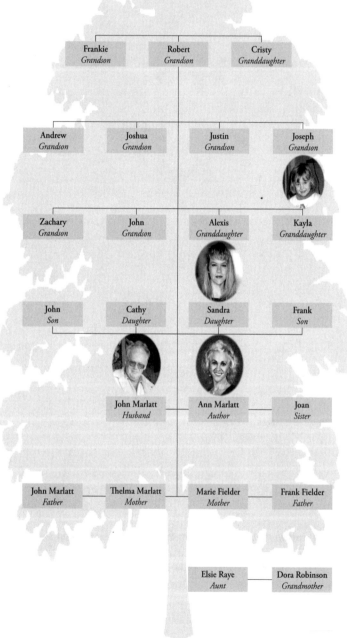

| Frankie | Robert | Cristy |
| Grandson | Grandson | Granddaughter |

| Andrew | Joshua | Justin | Joseph |
| Grandson | Grandson | Grandson | Grandson |

| Zachary | John | Alexis | Kayla |
| Grandson | Grandson | Granddaughter | Granddaughter |

| John | Cathy | Sandra | Frank |
| Son | Daughter | Daughter | Son |

| John Marlatt | Ann Marlatt | Joan |
| Husband | Author | Sister |

| John Marlatt | Thelma Marlatt | Marie Fielder | Frank Fielder |
| Father | Mother | Mother | Father |

| Elsie Raye | Dora Robinson |
| Aunt | Grandmother |

Story Twenty

If we allow ourselves to stay open to the possibilities of life, we may get unexpected confirmation that a loved one who has crossed over is still with us and trying to let us know that he or she is okay.

I always knew my dad was still around. I could feel him when I walked into a room or just before I fell asleep at night. My two-year-old daughter, an extremely bright and very talkative little girl, was the last grandchild and, as all of his grandchildren were, an apple of my dads' eye. "Not now Kayla!" I must have heard Dad say those words a hundred times. Kayla always had a different idea. From the moment she was able to crawl she would find him and demand that he hold her and love her. She followed him around like a puppy. From the first thing in the morning to the last thing she did at night, Grandpa was her world. They were inseparable. Dad was so weak, it took all the strength he had to even take a few steps. Kayla would not leave him alone. She stayed right on his heels. She seemed to know instinctively what he needed. If Grandpa left the house without her, she would cry for him.

Christmas was a very big time of year at Mom and Dad's house. It was a miracle to see what child or entire family would show up in their lives in the late December days in need of a little love and a little Christmas. Dad was never happier than when he would have to rush out to the store to bring the needed gifts of love to a family in need. There was Christmas dinner to be supplied, new clothes and a warm coat for the children who otherwise would have been as cold as the winter season that filled the air. And it goes without mentioning, there was always a toy or two wrapped in bright Christmas paper for the big morning. They knew they couldn't help everyone in the world, but for Mom and especially Dad, it was a way to give thanks for all the blessings in their lives. Many of those families never knew where the blessing came from, they were just told to say thank you to God, and a seed was planted for them to keep the blessing alive by helping someone else along the way when they were able.

It was just such a time. It was only days until Christmas. Dad was ill, yet there he was dragging his oxygen tanks up to his motorized cart to do some last minute shopping for a family in need. We would offer to go along to help but it was something he wanted to do by himself. "If I die shopping I will die a happy man," he would say. When he arrived home, I went out to unload the treasures that he had brought for our family, as well as what would be the last family that would ever be blessed by my parents again, for this was to be Dad's last Christmas for us and to the world. "I found this doll," he told me, "it looks so much like Kayla; something inside of me just couldn't pass it by. I had to have it for her."

Dad and I spoke about all the wonderful times we had together over the years. He shared with me that he felt it would be the last time he would celebrate the holidays with the family he loved so much. I laughed and cried as I looked at the little bundle in the special box. I knew it would probably be the last gift that Kayla would receive from her grandpa.

"Dad," I asked, "would it be ok if I put this doll away for another time? Kayla is only a year old and she will not be able to appreciate what this gift means." Dad smiled and then agreed. We decided to keep this a little secret between the two of us, a special father-daughter moment in time. I took the little doll to storage where all the rest of my belongings were placed till my husband and I could buy a home of our own.

As he had predicted, Dad passed away before we had another holiday to celebrate together. The following Christmas Eve, the memory of the doll suddenly struck my heart. It would be the perfect time to deliver the gift, I thought. It would be a gift for the both of us. Kayla would receive the doll and I would feel like Dad was still with us this Christmas morning. I got the little doll out of storage, dusted off the box and wrapped it in bright red and green paper. The secret of the gift would be forever locked in my heart. I would tell no one.

It was weeks later. Kayla was enjoying herself, laughing, talking and playing with her doll. All that giggling made me go and check on her. I wondered if there was someone else in the house.

"Kayla, you sure seem to be happy playing with your doll," I told her. "Who are you talking to back here?"

"Grandpa," said Kayla.

"Really? Tell me about playing with Grandpa."

"Grandpa said that my new doll was a special present from him. He said he got it for me. He said to ask you about it, Mommy. Did he Mommy? Did my grandpa give me this special doll for Christmas?"

"Yes Kayla, Grandpa did get that baby doll for you. It was his special gift just for you. Has Grandpa come to play with you before?"

"Yes," she said, "Grandpa comes and plays with me all the time. Mostly we play with my baby doll. Sometimes he comes to play with me and takes me to his house in the clouds. He likes to run up the stairs in his house because he said he couldn't run when he was sick. He hides behind the clouds but I always find him. Sometime Alexis comes to play with us, too. We laugh and laugh."

She told me about Grandpa's daddy who comes to play with them sometimes, too. "That's my other grandpa that plays with us in the clouds," she said as we were sorting through a pile of old photos. Kayla never met her great-grandpa so it came as a big surprise to me when she pointed him out.

How I loved to share in those special times that she was experiencing with her Grandpa. It kept me feeling so close to my dad, but time moves on and Kayla will soon be a teenager. When we speak about the blessing of her wonderful time with her grandpa she has a puzzled look on her face. She has lost the innocence of a younger Kayla and now wonders how this could have happened. The joy she experienced of that special time with Grandpa is now just a story that she hears repeated during times when the family gets together and we reminisce about my dad. Maybe it was planned to happen just the way it did or maybe dad used the special secret between the two of us as a way to let me know that he was still just as much apart of our lives as he ever was. I miss him so.

As much as I tried to help Kayla keep the memory of her visits with her grandpa alive she sadly admitted to me one day that she no longer remembers anything that happened. She was sad because she wanted me to be happy and she felt that her memory of the events would make me happy that grandpa was still in our lives. My daughter Sandra says she can feel John around her at times. I have not felt or had any contact with John since my dream but somehow I know that he is with me.

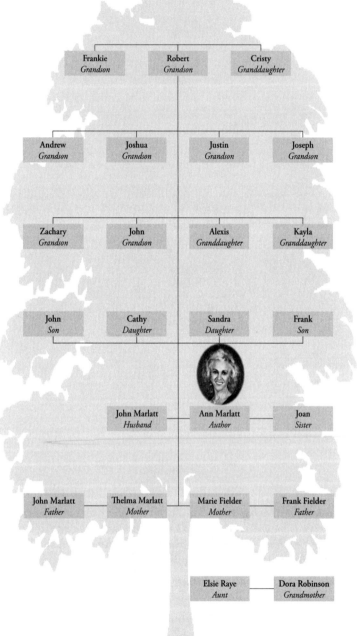

Story Twenty-One

Divine intervention can bring miracles to our lives that we will never even be aware of. After this incident, I wondered how many miracles I have had in my own life.

It started out like a usual week day morning. Mornings were all mine since I worked afternoons and I always preferred to start the day with my walk. This morning was nothing out of the ordinary as I stepped out of the door with all the usual gear: some upbeat music to keep me moving and a walking stick to keep the dogs away, the two and the four-legged kind. I headed up the street to follow one of my usual routes. I changed my path routinely for a variety of reasons but there were places that I would never walk alone. One of those places was a road called Granite Hill.

It was an access road that ran next to the freeway but something spooked me out of walking there. I could never quite put my finger on it, but I was always nervous when I walked in that area. There was a fence between the road and the freeway and the other side was empty hills. Sometimes the road narrowed between two granite rocks to an area with no shoulder. Sometimes because of the up and down hills, you could not see more than a few feet ahead. Some people thought nothing of dumping their rubbish and trash in its isolated valleys, and I knew that a body or two had been found in the area. Perhaps it was the wild dogs and coyotes that I spotted occasionally. It was just too isolated to be safe; there was no place to go should you need to get away. Several years before I decided to listen to that little inner voice that rang out a warning and made it a point never to walk there alone.

So why in the world after all these years did I find myself heading for Granite Hill? I knew I didn't want to walk there. I kept thinking about the isolation of the road and telling myself to turn around and go back. Something just kept driving me on. When I reached the road I stood there for what seems like the longest time. Every fiber of my being wanted to turn back, but something bigger just kept urging me forward. I decided to go left, or did I? I realized I hadn't decided anything. I just went that way. I cannot even begin to express how uncomfortable I was feeling, and yet I felt helpless to stop myself. As I walked farther down the road I thought about how committed I was now to getting to the next overcrossing. I began to pick up my pace. I felt like a crazy woman arguing with myself out there. Telling myself that I was either going to be attacked by something, or some other horrible thing was going to befall me because I was acting so stupidly. I was really afraid. Why in the world had I put myself in this position where all my senses felt like I was approaching danger?

I spotted a couple of children on bikes and thought, I am not totally alone at this moment. It gave me a momentary sense of relief. After they passed, the bad feeling returned. I began to imagine all kinds of horrible scenarios. Maybe some crazy maniac was waiting around the next rock to hit me in the head, or some pack of wild dogs was waiting to rip my throat out. I was more than half way down that road now and couldn't wait to reach the overpass. "Never again am I going to put myself in this position," I muttered. I started to walk between a narrowed area. Some large boulders had been blasted away to put the road in. There was no shoulder on each side of the narrow road and it was impossible to see up and over for approaching traffic. I was being especially careful as I walked. I got to the top of the area and noticed how someone had dumped trash along the roadside. There were clothes and toys and other belongings. I thought it must have been there for a time because it was covered with dirt from the winds that blew the past few nights. I spotted what I thought was some kind of homemade toy. But for the life of me, I couldn't figure out what kind of a toy it could be.

"Must have been dumped with this other stuff," I thought. But something made me stop and look at it again. What is this thing? It was not covered with dirt like all the rest of the junk laying here. I realized that it must have been placed there earlier that morning after the winds had stopped blowing. I stood there just looking at it in amazement. It was a 12" piece of galvanized pipe about 1" in diameter. One end was caped and wrapped with duct tape. The other end had a 12" stick like a piece of broom handle or a dowel stick. It looked as though it was chopped with an ax to make it splintered several inches down. It was wrapped with duct tape around the entry point in the pipe. I saw a screw going through the pipe and it looked like it was all the way through to the ground but I wasn't sure. I started to move it with my walking stick when I felt a voice in my mind say, "Stop! If you move it, you will blow off your legs!" My senses would not allow me to believe the thing I was looking at was a real bomb. People just don't find bombs sitting along the roadside. Why would anyone put a bomb here? I studied it for a very long time. My mind would not believe what my eyes were seeing. I decided that my over-active imagination was still running away with me. This is probably some kid's toy. Forget it, I thought. I'm nearly to the overcrossing, I am just going to walk home. I started to walk away and the strangest feeling came over me. I turned back and looked at it again.

Suddenly another message came into my head. "If you walk away without doing something about this, a child will lose his life today." A chill ran down my spine. What if this is true? What if I was sent down this road for some kind of Divine intervention? I wrestled with that for a long time. Still I could find no other earthly explanation as to why I was so compelled to be there.

I looked up and saw another group of children riding bikes in the distance. They turned toward the overpass. I pondered what to do now. I had no phone and where the heck were those cops that use to follow me now? I saw a police car on the other side of the freeway and tried to wave him down but he was too far away. I started to pray. It was impressed on my mind that I must act, even if I couldn't believe that this was really happening. It suddenly occurred to me that if this was a bomb, somebody could be watching my actions. Should I stay here and wait and possibly become a target for some crazy person, or should I try to make it into town and call 911? I suddenly had a sense of urgency. I started to run towards town. If this was a bomb I had to be quick. The thought of one of those children dying was more than I could bear. I prayed that I would not be too late to make a difference.

I got into town and stopped at one of the local merchants. I told them what was happening and I called 911. The person on the other end of the phone must have thought I was a crank caller. He began to question me.

"Lady, how do you know what a bomb looks like?"

"I don't know," I said.

"What makes you think this is a bomb?"

"I don't know," I said.

"Did you put something there in the roadway?"

He was not taking my call seriously. He really had me on the defensive. I think he wanted me to hang up and go away. *I* couldn't believe I came across a bomb on the side of the road, why should I think the police would take me seriously? I was getting absolutely nowhere with him. I prayed for the right thing to say to get through to him.

"Please sir, could you spell your name for me," I suddenly asked.

"Why?" he replied.

"I want to be sure to get it right when I call the news team tonight and report that you allowed a child to be killed today when you refused to take my call seriously." He was quiet for a time and then seemed a little short when dealing with me. He told me, "Stay where you are, an officer will be there shortly to assist you."

I added, "Hurry!"

I felt like a criminal as I was stuffed into the back of that squad car. We drove the mile or so back to the area. I pointed out the object and she said that it indeed looked a little suspicious. She got down on her hands and knees and her nose was nearly touching it. She was blowing the dirt around from beneath it when I stepped back and said, "Is it really worth getting your face blown off if that thing really is a bomb?" Deciding it was a good possibility that this thing was real, she called for back up. The special unit bomb team decided that the bomb could not safely be moved from the area so the freeway was closed down in both directions while they blew it up on the site. I was told it was not only a pipe bomb, but a big pipe bomb.

The newspaper reported that the walking lady found the explosive devise during her daily walk in that area. "It's a good thing that she walks up there regularly," they all said. "No telling what would have happened if some child would have found it first." I knew differently. I fought my own emotions and wrestled with my own fears to walk Granite Hill road that day. I had no idea what I was doing there. Devine intervention prevented a tragedy. I was more amazed by that then the fact that I found the bomb in the first place. I know in my heart that God's Divine Intervention saved a child who will grow up and never realize the blessing that was given to him and his family that day. I couldn't help but wonder how many blessings we all have in our lives that we will never know about.

The bomb was found on Granite Hill road, Glen Avon California, in the late 1990's.

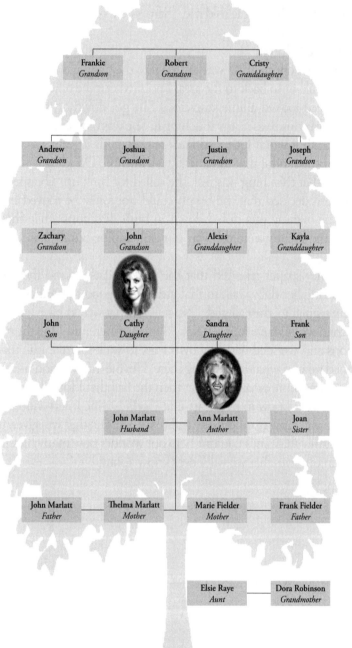

Frankie
Grandson

Robert
Grandson

Cristy
Granddaughter

Andrew
Grandson

Joshua
Grandson

Justin
Grandson

Joseph
Grandson

Zachary
Grandson

John
Grandson

Alexis
Granddaughter

Kayla
Granddaughter

John
Son

Cathy
Daughter

Sandra
Daughter

Frank
Son

John Marlatt
Husband

Ann Marlatt
Author

Joan
Sister

John Marlatt
Father

Thelma Marlatt
Mother

Marie Fielder
Mother

Frank Fielder
Father

Elsie Raye
Aunt

Dora Robinson
Grandmother

Story Twenty-Two

Life can be very painful. You feel that you can't go on another day. You want the pain to stop but you see no hope in sight. This angelic visit may bring hope back to your life, too.

I could never put into words how I was feeling that night. The emotional and spiritual pain from a failing marriage caused me to toss and turn until one in the morning. It was useless for me to stay in bed any longer. I needed a place to be alone to think and try to find some kind of peace with what was happening in my life. The house was still and quiet as I wandered room to room to check on my children. Fearing my restlessness might awaken them I decided to slip outside and sit in my car. I was at my breaking point, fearful I would slip over the edge and if I did, I was afraid I would never come back. I have never felt so alone.

I turned on the radio in my car and listened to a Christian broadcast hoping to find some kind of answers, some kind of message that would help me get through the night. I don't think that I ever prayed as hard as I was praying that night, begging God to intervene in my life. I began to cry uncontrollably and just couldn't stop. I looked up to the clear star-filled night and pleaded with God for help. I cast my eyes downward to wipe the tears and then back up to continue my prayer but instead of the night stars and sky, my eye focused on what I thought was a hallucination. I looked back down, shook myself off, and looked back up. I was totally overwhelmed. It was so huge I couldn't believe my eyes. There was a throne sitting on the top of our roof. Our house was 80 feet long with a very pitched roof. The throne was at least 30 feet wide.

It stood so high that it blocked the view of the large eucalyptus tree in the backyard that grew tall above the roof. It had four legs, two resting on one side of the roof and two on the other. The throne had such intricate detail. At the bottom of the legs and the ends of the arms were the carved paws of a lion or a bear, , each one different. But the most awesome part was what was sitting on that throne and looking straight at me. It was some kind of an angel. I can't describe how beautiful this creature was. It had long dark hair down to about the waist. I could not tell if it was male or female by its appearance or its voice. It was wearing the most beautiful robe, tied at the waist with some kind of a rope. The color was nothing like I have ever seen before. I can only describe it as pure. The robe shined with a pure brilliant light. I don't know how, but I seemed to be able to see through it to the back of the throne. It had huge wings and the throne was carved to accommodate them.

I couldn't stop staring at it and it kept its eyes focused on me. Then it began to speak to me. I was amazed by the fact that we never opened our mouths to talk. The words just seem to come from our minds. As we spoke our eye contact never stopped. I felt as though we might be speaking through our eyes and from our minds. The sight of it was the most powerful thing that had ever happened in my life. I could feel the awesome power in its voice as it spoke and yet it was so soft and gentle, soothing and pure. I had a feeling of total trust.

It spoke with much expression. Although its lips never, moved it used many hand gestures while it spoke to me. I told it how frightened I was, afraid that I was going to lose my mind. It softly and gently conveyed understanding of my feelings. It told me that things were going to get really difficult in my life for about five to six years. I tried to ask what was going to happen but it would not give me the slightest hint of what was going to occur. It just kept telling me that I had to be strong. Over and over it made a point of repeating the message of how life would be a challenge and even though I felt like I could not get through it, I was going to be okay. "Hold on to your faith," it said, "you will not be alone."

I wanted more. There were so many questions that I wanted to ask of this beautiful angel, but I felt like I was somehow purposely distracted from asking. It stayed with me for more than half an hour. It brought me more comfort in that time than I have ever experienced in my life. We spoke about the beautiful throne where it sat with its wings fitted so perfectly into the carved area in the back. I said it was the most beautiful thing I had ever seen. It shared with me that what was carved on that throne was every living thing that God created on the earth. With all my soul I wanted to stay in that moment forever. But as quickly as it appeared to me, it was gone. Part of me was finally at peace and yet I was terrified of what the next few years would bring. I found comfort in the knowledge that I would always be watched over and now I know that angels would always be around me.

Cathy has had many challenges in her life over these past years but she still holds onto the words of faith that were given to her by an angel on a throne.

Frankie	Robert	Cristy
Grandson	*Grandson*	*Granddaughter*

Andrew	Joshua	Justin	Joseph
Grandson	*Grandson*	*Grandson*	*Grandson*

Zachary	John	Alexis	Kayla
Grandson	*Grandson*	*Granddaughter*	*Granddaughter*

John	Cathy	Sandra	Frank
Son	*Daughter*	*Daughter*	*Son*

John Marlatt	Ann Marlatt	Joan
Husband	*Author*	*Sister*

John Marlatt	Thelma Marlatt	Marie Fielder	Frank Fielder
Father	*Mother*	*Mother*	*Father*

Elsie Raye	Dora Robinson
Aunt	*Grandmother*

Story Twenty-Three

When it's difficult to find something in life to be thankful for, the answer could be to just be thankful for life.

Mom and I decided to at least try and make the effort to celebrate Thanksgiving, despite all the sadness surrounding our lives. In happier times Thanksgiving dinner was the most family-oriented time of the year. I thought about the time that Dad purchased an old salad bar from a restaurant that was replacing it with a newer model. He proudly brought it home to Mom and told her that this should solve all of our storage problems for the 70 or more people we prepared a feast for each year. They grew their own vegetables and even raised the turkey. I told Mom that I had a small check to cash at the bank and then I would go to the market. I planned on buying a small turkey and the needed baking ingredients for her to make the pumpkin pies.

I left my daughter Cristy in the open-aired Jeepster with a friend while I went into the Wells Fargo Bank. The line was so long that day. I was sad that I felt less than joy about what I had to be thankful for that year. My mind went back to happier times when we were really celebrating the joy of being together. A tear welled up in my eye as a cherished memory crossed my mind about the time that our turkey was so big it kept pushing the oven door open with its legs. I remembered how Dad laughed and finally braced that chair against the oven door to keep it closed.

My eyes began to wander about, wondering how each person would be celebrating the holiday. Some in the bank seemed to be so rushed and annoyed, and there were others who couldn't care less about what it took to make this a joyous time. I turned my eyes toward the outside glass door and noticed the two men standing there and wondered how they were going to celebrate. As I observed them I began to get a terrible feeling in the pit of my stomach. They were very nervous. They both took a cigarette from a pack and lit up. They sucked so hard on those cigarettes I thought that the cigarette would burn up and explode. As they put the cigarettes out they looked up at me and stared into my eyes. A sudden feeling came over me and I knew what was about to happen. A voice from somewhere deep within me began to scream in my head. "Get out of here now!" I was trying to make my feet move but was finding it nearly impossible.

Finally I took a deep breath and stepped backwards out of the line. The two men stood there watching me, never taking their eyes off of me. They pulled ski masks out from their jacket pocket and put them over their heads to cover their faces. I knew I was in real trouble now. The door flew open and they yelled, "Freeze!" I was already frozen to the floor. They yelled for everybody except the tellers to get down on the floor. I could not move. One of the men took the clip that he carried in his hand and shoved it into the 45 that he was holding. He pulled pack the lever to engage the bullet into the chamber. I knew what was about to be my fate. The gun was pointed straight at me from only a few feet away. A bank clerk began to scream.

"Oh my God," she said, "he's going to kill her. Oh God, she is going to die. No, no" she screamed.

The first man told her to shut up. I was trying desperately to cover my head and trunk with my arms; it was the only move I seem to be able to make. I could see beyond the mask into his eyes. I knew every mark on his face, it just seem to be etched into my mind. I saw the look of determination and knew that he felt killing me would be the only way to protect his identity. Everything seemed to be moving in slow motion now. I watched as he squeezed the trigger and heard the click of the hammer hitting its mark but nothing happened. The gun suddenly came apart. The clip fell to the floor. I heard the teller scream again at the top of her lungs. I watched as the man bent over to get the clip and shove it back into the gun. Suddenly something jerked me towards the door. I just knew that I was flying in that direction.

I swear to this day I don't remember my feet touching the floor until I was outside. I grabbed my daughter by the arm and tried to flip her out of the Jeepster. Her seat belt was on and she screamed. I yelled for her to get it loose. My friend was laughing and playfully yelled out, "Wow, you look like you just robbed the bank."

I was screaming, "Run! Run!" We took off down the strip mall to a store. I used the phone to call 911. The bank clerks were never able to hit the silent alarm button and my call was the only notification that was given to the police. They asked me to go outside and see if they had come out of the bank. I saw them leave and reported so to the police.

I spent the next half hour or so frozen in time. I was still in a state of shock as I finally walked back to my car. I was so shaken by the incident that I decided I was not going to go back into the bank when I heard a familiar voice screaming. It was the teller. She was yelling, "It's her, it's her! That's the woman. They tried to kill her. They fired the gun and the gun just fell apart. She was dead, I just knew she was a dead woman."

The police and the FBI ran out the door to my car. I must have been in shock, I felt so calm on the outside and all I wanted to do is scream and run on the inside. "Miss," inquired one of the men, "were you the woman that called about the bank robbery?"

"Yes," I replied.

"Please come back in the bank, we need to ask you some questions." I told them I had to go to the store. Mom had to make the pies. I guess it was pretty silly but you just seem to think of the dumbest things when faced with traumatic circumstances. I was asked if I could identify the two men who robbed the bank. I told them I could see every detail of their faces and why. It seems that I was the only one who really saw them. I told them about the cigarettes and they were able to retrieve them for DNA evidence. They sent for a police artist to draw the two men while the picture of them was still fresh in my mind. We were there for hours. My daughter began to complain about being hungry. They went and got us food. Needless to say, I wasn't thinking much about eating. I remember telling them that I had to call my mom. "She is going to wonder what happened to us." They gave me a phone. "Hello Mom, we are okay and I will explain when I get home." I left her in a panic, wondering if we had been in an accident or what happened in the past few hours.

The bank had been closed immediately after the robbery. I looked down at the little crumpled up check in my hand that I came into the bank to cash earlier. My mind raced through the miracles that saved me that day. I thought about what I was thinking when I came into the bank earlier. What did I have to be so thankful for this year? God answered that question for me now. I have my life and my children will have their mother.

"I don't suppose you could cash my check?" I said as I tried to smooth out the wrinkled mess of paper in my hand. "My mom is waiting at home to make the pies." They laughed and took the check from my hand. I looked at the teller who took it from me. "After all of this, I sure hope the check is good. It's from my ex-husband."

The bank robbery was at the Wells Fargo Bank that was on Mission Blvd, Glen Avon, California. The bank has since been closed down and is now a pawnshop. So many people have asked her about that check from her ex husband. They have wondered if it was worth what she went through that day at the bank. She smiles and says you be the judge, the check was for $100. and yes, it was good.

Frankie	Robert	Cristy
Grandson	*Grandson*	*Granddaughter*

Andrew	Joshua	Justin	Joseph
Grandson	*Grandson*	*Grandson*	*Grandson*

Zachary	John	Alexis	Kayla
Grandson	*Grandson*	*Granddaughter*	*Granddaughter*

John	Cathy	Sandra	Frank
Son	*Daughter*	*Daughter*	*Son*

John Marlatt	Ann Marlatt	Joan
Husband	*Author*	*Sister*

John Marlatt	Thelma Marlatt	Marie Fielder	Frank Fielder
Father	*Mother*	*Mother*	*Father*

Elsie Raye	Dora Robinson
Aunt	*Grandmother*

Story Twenty-Four

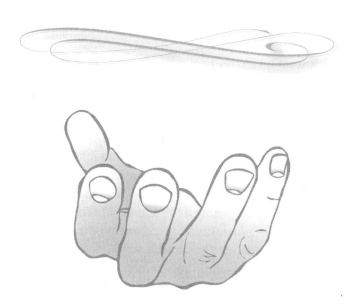

Everything seemed to be moving in slow motion as Frank witnessed the events of the freak accident unfolding before his eyes.

The day began ordinarily enough. I was planning on running an errand or two and then dropping off my nieces and nephew at their grandparent's house.

"Come on, sis," I yelled out, "I need to get going. I want to get back before dark."

The kids were finally ready and heading for the door when Cathy came out from the back room. "I've changed my mind," she said. "I will take the kids to their grandparent's house later this evening." She began to say something about having a bad feeling about the kids going with me but I was just annoyed by the unnecessary delay and didn't pay much attention to what she was trying to say to me. "You just go ahead and run your errands and hurry back, but please be careful."

The freeway traffic was terrible that day so I decided to get off and take the side streets. I was cresting a hill and on my way down when the incredible nightmare began. Everything seemed to be moving in slow motion as I witnessed the events of this freak accident unfolding before my eyes, knowing that there was nothing I could do to stop it.

Going downhill and around a curve at about 50 or 60 mph the old beat up truck hit the concrete drainage ditch on the side of the road after it blew a front tire. I watched the truck begin to roll, not side-to-side but up on its front end. The truck was standing on its nose and about to go over, hanging in the air as if by some invisible suspension that picked it up from the rear. I could see clearly into the cab of the pick-up truck and saw the man in the front seat, frozen in fear. I was frightened beyond words at the sudden realization that the man I was watching, was me. Somehow after the tire blew and I lost control of the truck I was ejected from my body. I was hovering above the truck watching the incredible events unfold. I could see the truck with me inside the cab begin to roll over on its top. Suddenly from nowhere a huge hand appeared and broke out the back window between the cab and the bed of the truck.

I watched as this hand reached in and pulled me out through the opening before the truck landed on its top. The hand pushed me down in the bed of the truck and held me there as the truck began a slide down the hill. Oh God, pain! It was the first realization that I had somehow been thrown back into my body. When the truck finally stopped, my leg was pinned and my face was on fire from sliding on the ground beneath the truck. I was hurting, but I was alive and my injuries were not life threatening.

After getting free, I stood looking at that old pick-up truck and was terrified to see what was left of the cab. It was completely crushed to the seat and floor. I thought about what could have happened to my nieces and nephew if they had been with me, had it not been for a sudden impulse on my sister's part. "I just had a feeling that they shouldn't go with you today."

The accident occurred on Sierra Blvd at the San Bernardino and Riverside county line. The truck was a total loss. Frank's injuries were not severe but they are very lasting. He continues to have problems with that knee to this day.

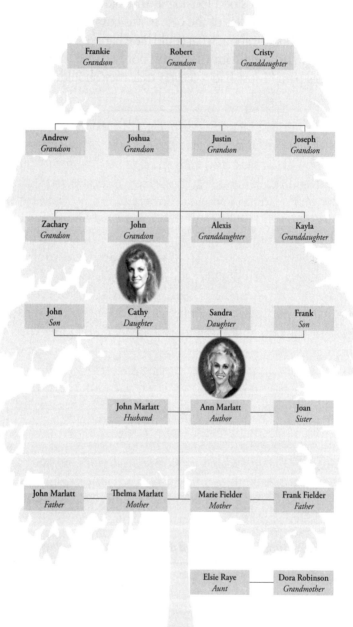

| Frankie
Grandson | Robert
Grandson | Cristy
Granddaughter |

| Andrew
Grandson | Joshua
Grandson | Justin
Grandson | Joseph
Grandson |

| Zachary
Grandson | John
Grandson | Alexis
Granddaughter | Kayla
Granddaughter |

| John
Son | Cathy
Daughter | Sandra
Daughter | Frank
Son |

| John Marlatt
Husband | Ann Marlatt
Author | Joan
Sister |

| John Marlatt
Father | Thelma Marlatt
Mother | Marie Fielder
Mother | Frank Fielder
Father |

| Elsie Raye
Aunt | Dora Robinson
Grandmother |

Story Twenty-Five

God……... I made it.

It was more than eight years since my promise to do a marathon. With the years came the blessing of better health than I had ever known, but John's death left me emotionally and spiritually drained. I am not sure if it was my promise to God that made me face life again or facing life again that made me think about my promise, but now it began to weigh heavily on my heart. I could not shake the feeling that I was letting myself down by not keeping my word but I didn't have a clue how to go about achieving such an impossible goal. I couldn't even imagine taking on such a huge physical challenge. I thought about asking God to just let me off the hook. I was a grandmother over 50 years old. Who would blame me if I felt the time had passed to be able to do a marathon? I'm too old, I'm too weak, I'm too big, it's just too late, and the whole ordeal was just too big a challenge in the first place. God, I need answers, I prayed. I don't know what to do, I don't know how to do it, or if I should even try to do it.

Within days, an unsolicited flyer arrived in my mailbox. It advertised a training course in how to complete a marathon. I read about the training sessions that would require many months of dedication to a rigorous schedule and instructions on who to contact to apply for participation in the San Diego Marathon the following year. I knew down to my very soul that this was a promise that God wanted me to keep. All the terrible "too's" were stripped away in a heartbeat. I had many fears and uncertainties about my own abilities, but I knew that it was more than coincidence that this was happening. I was going to have to suck it up, put my fears aside and believe that anything can be accomplished in my life, even what seemed to be impossible.

The lady on the other end of the phone was wonderful and reassuring as we spoke about the details of the marathon. "How long will they leave the finish line up?" I asked. "I have this vision of me alone, in the scorching sun, face down, my mouth swollen, parched and bleeding, crawling across the hot blowing sand of some far off desert, barely able to speak and begging them not to take down the finish line." When we both stopped laughing she assured me that the finish line would not come down until the last participant had finished, no matter how long it took.

The classes met every Saturday morning. There were days when it was a hoot to feel so good, and to be out there training and keeping up with these young marathon hopefuls. It was such a blessing to be able to put one foot in front of the other for such long distances. But there were also harder times when the demands of the training brought me to my knees, and more times than I care to remember that I found myself nearly passing out in the street. I traveled some for work and pleasure during those months, but I still planned for and kept to my schedule. The training was the greatest physical, emotional, and spiritual challenge of my life. Once on an airplane two hours after completing a 13-mile training session, I found myself hopelessly anchored to the seat with my legs cramped so tightly that I could not get up. I learned a new lesson that day: don't run, jog, and walk 13 miles, take a hot shower, and then get on a plane without room to stretch your legs and expect to get up and move around.

"The months passed quickly," said my daughter as she and a friend accompanied me to the marathon registration area. "I'm in the best shape of my life," I said, "but is it going to be good enough to finish the 26.2 miles tomorrow?"

It was an unforgettable moment to pick up my registration packet with my official participant number. The realization of how far I had come over the past few years began to filter into my consciousness. Just being there filled me with a sense of excitement more wonderful than I have ever known. I was spending the night in my motor home in the mall parking lot near the starting area. I was taking no chances that something would prevent me from standing at the starting line on time in the morning.

I don't know how much I really slept that night, but despite my restlessness the hours passed quickly. I felt numb now as I finished getting ready and went out to join the waiting crowd. The still dark pre-dawn sky was beautifully clear and unusually warm for this time of the year. I was hypnotized by the twinkling of millions of far off stars that filled the darkness as I walked toward the banner high above the crowd that read "San Diego Marathon Starting Line." I was more excited and tense than I thought I would be. I tried to imagine how I would be feeling standing in this same place the next night. The most challenging day of my life would begin here in just a few short moments and then, like a thousand other days, it would be gone. There were spectators everywhere yelling and cheering for all of us waiting for our moment to begin. I glanced towards my daughter and friend waving and cheering for me. I was suddenly impacted by the fact that I was really doing this. I became momentarily lost in my thoughts, and it frightened me to remember how sick I had been so many years before.

My health had been restored and I was here celebrating the miracles that happened for my life. I suddenly realized that it didn't matter what happened today because the unbelievable victory for my life had already been won, just by being here. The noise of the screaming crowd brought me back to the present. Time seemed to be moving in slow motion now and the tension grew as the moment came close to begin. Did a gun go off? I wasn't sure…I was just suddenly aware that the crowd of participants began to move. I tried to take my first step but found myself hopelessly frozen to the ground. I asked God to help me find my feet, and after a little spiritual shove I was on my way. The thrill of that first step was indescribable and my momentary sense of the overwhelming was replaced by the thoughts of all that I learned during my training. It was still dark and difficult to see. There were guides on roller skates among us with lights shining down on the path that lit the way in the dark so we wouldn't trip and fall. You never know when an epiphany is going to open your eyes. I reflected on all the circumstances that brought me to this day and pondered the possibility of guides and angels of my own shining lights on my path. All through the grueling months of training I really thought I was alone in my efforts and I never really gave consideration to the fact that I was never alone.

It was a beautiful morning as I moved along with the others. The sight of the sun's first light rising over the calm ocean water was beautiful, but it also seemed to have a sobering effect on the day at hand. The first few miles dragged on forever. I was surprised to be feeling so sluggish. I finally grabbed an energy bar and a cup of water and shortly thereafter I found my stride. I was on a roll now. It was the uphill section of the marathon and my pace was good. When I crested the top of the hill and started back down I reached the sign that announced the halfway point. I was well within the time that I was hoping for and now it was all downhill for the next few miles. I was moving with a huge adrenaline rush. I was halfway there and running like the wind, or at least a good strong breeze. I was jazzed and felt unstoppable, singing with the music in my headphones when the unbelievable horrible stinging pain first hit. The bottom of my foot was on fire as a huge blister that had formed over the past 16 miles burst. It was like a nightmare. The pain was so intense that it stopped me cold in my tracks. I thought I could just run it off but the pain continued to intensify. It slowed my pace to a moderate walk as I limped on the side of my foot. I took some Advil and continued down the line. The pain overtook my mind so intently that it became the only thing that I could think about. The distance seemed to become endless now. I had hit the wall, as they say, and I couldn't seem to recover my stride and concentration.

Around the twenty-first mile I decided to stop and try to readjust my sock to make it a little more comfortable and to slap some Vaseline on the bottom of my foot to soothe the raw nerve endings. I sat down on the edge of a wall and removed my shoe, but to my dismay I found the sock was so deeply imbedded in and around the ruptured blister that I could not remove it. I noticed that blood was coming from two of my toes and, from what I could feel through the sock, the nails were lifting, possibly with blisters under them as well. I took a deep breath and looked up to the sky. "You aren't going to make this easy on me, are you?" I said.

Suddenly I started to laugh as I began to sense the humor in this whole ordeal. I thought about the feelings I had earlier in the pre-dawn darkness about how I would feel standing at the starting line the next day. Giving up was never an issue but now I was more determined than ever not to let anything stop me just because the going got tough. This day was going to be gone very soon and blisters and pain were going to heal. I knew that what I did today, every decision I made and every step I took, would be with me for the rest of my life. I put my shoe back on and took off again. It would be a rather slow walk for a while but nothing was going to stop me. I happened to walk past a young man and woman whom I recognized from my training classes. He was crying and telling her that he couldn't go on. She was yelling at him because they were so close to finishing. I remembered during my training how I admired their youth and often thought about how much easier it was going to be for the two of them to do this marathon. My heart went out to him. I said a silent prayer that he would be able to find the courage to keep going.

Now all the wonder of what I was going to accomplish when I crossed that finish line came rushing to me. I smiled and laughed as I limped down the street like a wounded deer. I was truly learning a lot about myself out there that day. Spectators on the street were cheering and held up signs that kept us all encouraged as we made our way through the final three or four miles of the route. I remember a woman yelling from the sidelines, "Just think what you are accomplishing! You are among the elite." I was down to the 24-mile marker, just two miles to go. A second wind must have filled me because I just took off running again. The pain became the last thing on my mind. I was going to cross that finish line running. It was a small downhill area and I felt more incredible than I have ever felt in my life.

The one-mile to go sign caught my eye as I raced by. People were yelling and cheering and bands were playing. I could see the finish line just up ahead. I heard my name and looked over to see my daughter and my friend. I don't know who was crying harder - them or me. I was almost hysterical as I turned to them and they snapped my picture. The finish line was just a few feet away. I wanted to stop and take each step deliberately and slowly but I didn't want to lose my pace and hold up the other runners. It seemed in slow motion once again as my foot hit the carpet at the finish line and snapped the photo that I would come to cherish. "Oh my God," I yelled as loud as I could, "I finished! I did it." I didn't know what to do or where to turn. I was laughing and crying and walking in circles, overwhelmed by the incredible accomplishment of my life. Some one came up and reached out a hand of congratulations, then put a medal around my neck.

I was directed to the photo area to take the one last victory shot with my arms up in the air but I was just unable to get my arms up and step up on the stool at the same time. My daughter put a special chain around my neck. It had a charm that read "26.2 miles." "Oh God," I repeated over and over as I stood there sobbing. I made it to the end and crossed over the line. I was in a world of joy and accomplishment and I wanted to hang on to this moment for as long as I could. I turned back to glance at the finish line just one last time. But I was stopped in my tracks and a new meaning for my life was born from the experience. The other side of that banner didn't say "finish line," it read "starting line".

For the first time I realized that I just crossed over the finish line of life as I had known it. Today was the day for healing and new beginnings. I said a silent prayer of thanks to God and to all the angels that helped me get through this day, and my life, one step at a time. I looked to the heaven, smiled and told John, "I made it."

This was the San Diego Marathon. The year was 1999 and I was number 3406. The San Diego marathon is held yearly in Carlsbad, California in the month of January.